JUST GRAB THE DUST RAG

Confessions of a Deluded Zen Student Who Never
Learned a Thing

A Book of Zen Moments

Brenda Eshin Shoshanna

Dedication

This book is dedicated to all the wonderful teachers, family, friends and sangha members who have traveled the road with me. To all I offer deep thanks.

The book is also dedicated to unknown students, those searching in the hope that somehow these words and moments may be an aid or inspiration in stepping onto this ancient path.

Table of Contents

Thanks and Acknowledgments

Among the many teachers and sangha I have sat with over the years, I wish to thank and acknowledge Soen Nakagawa Roshi, Eido Shimano Roshi, Kyudo Roshi, Yamakawa Roshi, Charlotte Joko Beck, Robert Kennedy Roshi, Konrad Ryushin Marchaj Sensei, Sensei Geoffrey Shugen Arnold Sensei, Sara Birnbaum, Sheila Curtis, Michael Creeley, Jacques Van Engel, Haskel Fleishaker, Fujin, Peter Gamby, Edward Glassing, Michael Yukon Grody, Martin Hara, Anthony McKiernen, Min Pai, Vincent Piazza, Richard Schiffman, Bernard Starr, Jacques Van Engel, Constantin Wickenburg, and many, many more.

I wish to offer special thanks and acknowledgment to Daishin Pawel Wojtasik for his deep, abiding love and commitment to Zen practice and to helping others along the way. I also thank him for his contribution of a wonderful cover photo and for being a dedicated reader as this book was being written, and offering unflagging encouragement and support.

I also thank Noah Lukeman and Adam Lukeman for their unfailing assistance in helping this book become available and fully realized.

Foreword

THIS BOOK IS A HISTORY of one student's many years of Zen practice. It is not intended as a history of the zendo or an exposé. Many of the events that have transpired are not recorded. The book is not a social commentary, nor does it claim to provide any ultimate truths about the teachings of Buddha. This is simply a book of Zen moments, the experience of practice with wonderful Japanese Zen asters and dedicated students, or sangha. The book wishes to convey the richness and beauty of Zen practice, along with inevitable foibles and confusion.

Much has been written about the Zen practice and the difficulties it gave rise to. Most of these writings look at Zen from a sociological, psychological and moral point of view. This book offers a look at practice through a different lens; it attempts to view events and interactions from the point of view of Zen practice and teachings. Hopefully, it rounds out the picture and adjusts some distortions that have developed.

This is simply the experience of one slow student who stayed forever, loved the zendo and all it offered, and found great treasures and riches in it. She saw great healing there for many, along with trouble and discord. She also saw the incredible efforts and dedication of the teachers to bring this practice to the West, along with their failings. The full picture needs to be recorded. That which was greatly meaningful and beautiful need not be wiped away.

Introduction

ONE AFTERNOON, WHEN I WAS FIFTEEN, a high school sophomore in Brooklyn, my history teacher motioned to me to stay after class. After everyone left, he slid over to me with something wrapped in brown paper in his hand. Obviously, he didn't want anyone else to see it.

"This is for you," he murmured under his breath. "Don't tell anybody. Take it home. I know you'll love it." Then he handed me the slim package.

Scared, I took it, tucked it under my arm and ran right home. Once safely inside, I went to my room, shut the door and closed the blinds. Then I opened the package. Inside was a little book titled *Studies In Zen* by D.T. Suzuki. This had to be a dangerous book, I thought, wondering why my teacher thought it was just right for me. Completely unaware of what it was about, I flipped through the pages and started to read.

Immediately, I was drawn in. Right from the start I came upon questions and answers that had taken place between ancient Zen masters and their students. These exchanges, called mondos and koans, were completely inscrutable. They didn't make any sense, were impossible to figure out. Smiling, I devoured every word of them. Even though I had no idea what any of it meant, waves of joy washed over me. The more I read the more I was filled with unexpected happiness. This is it! I thought, delighted. This is fantastic, amazing, I kept murmuring, with no idea why I was so happy at last.

Excited and thrilled, I put the book in my pocket and didn't let it go for years and years. Wherever I went, I took it with me and read it over again. When people asked what it was about, I said, "I have no idea." And I didn't, just couldn't stop reading the koans and mondos. I loved every one of them. When people asked what about it made me so happy, once again I said, "I have no idea." When they asked me what the koans meant, I didn't know, couldn't say a word. All I knew was that, in an instant, my whole life had turned around.

As the years went by I kept reading that book, but made no progress. I tried though. I poured over the inscrutable questions, dwelt upon them, read other people's commentaries, even wrote poems about them at the beach. But no matter what, I still didn't understand. And yet, whenever I engaged with these koans, my world opened wide. Emotional pain often quickly vanished and I learned what it meant to be a friend. Out of nowhere, life made sense. What kind of sense? Don't ask me. I don't understand.

Of course, when I suddenly married at age eighteen, the book came along with me down the aisle. Many times I asked my new husband if he thought my teacher would be coming to this country, or would I have to go to Japan?

"He's coming here," my husband reassured me, hoping I

would stop asking the same question and that this teacher I was hoping for would soon arrive.

Eleven years later I began hearing about a monk from Japan who was conducting sesshins—Zen meditation retreats—on the East Coast. When I first heard about him I was pregnant with my daughter. The man who told me about him had just returned from studying with him at a retreat. The man said I couldn't do zazen anyway because I was pregnant. He was wrong, but I listened to him.

Two years passed before I heard about this monk again. I was pregnant with my second child then, and at that time, actually living down the street from the zendo, which is a center for Zen meditation. The zendo was in the process of being built then. I passed the building every day, not realizing that the monk was right inside, giving every ounce of his energy to getting things ready for us to sit. Of course, I still didn't know I could do zazen when I was pregnant, so I didn't look into it any further then.

Four years later, and after the birth of my third child, I suddenly heard about this monk again. Now I knew the time was coming. I'd better get ready to go to the zendo and meet him, I thought. Before I went, though, I wanted someone to teach me how to do zazen.

Wado Vicky Gerdy appeared in my life just at that moment. We met in a class on sensory awareness and not only did she show me how to sit, she knew this monk personally, was part of the sangha (community) sitting with him. After one of our sensory awareness classes, we went into the dressing room and Vicky showed me how to do zazen in a quick offhand way.

I went home and tried. It was hard, it hurt, I squirmed, my knees stuck up and wouldn't go down into the cross-legged position. So I just did what I could each day. But what I couldn't understand was why even a little bit of sitting made each day so different. Or why, little by little, all by itself, my sittings grew longer, and my knees came down.

A few months later, I felt ready to go to the zendo, which was in a beautiful townhouse in Manhattan, on the Upper East Side. Thursday night was beginner's night. So, on a cool, lovely Thursday evening in autumn, along with other new students, I lined up outside the zendo. With excited anticipation, we all waited for the doors to open. Who knew what would happen then?

ॐ ॐ

AT EXACTLY 6:15—NOT A MINUTE sooner or later—the doors opened and the line started to move. The doors stayed open for forty-five minutes and closed at precisely 7 p.m. If you arrived at 7:01 the doors remained closed. No matter what you did then, you couldn't get in. Time mattered here.

The minute you entered the small vestibule, you were told to take off your shoes and put them into the shoe rack, *carefully*. Don't throw them in helter-skelter. Right from the beginning, pay attention, be aware. The way you treat your shoes is the way you treat everything else in your life. Messy shoes, messy mind!

If it was your first time here, you were directed upstairs to the second floor. As you climbed the steep stairway, the exquisite smell of incense followed you.

The students who were here for the first time were ushered into a large room and told to sit on the floor on round black cushions, and wait. Wait for what? No one knew. We crossed our legs awkwardly, straightened our backs, and waited. And, even though we were told to keep our eyes down, out of the corner of our eyes, we peeked at each other. Vinny was there, Harold, Sara, two Catholic nuns, and a few others. Oddly enough, this particular group kept returning for years, became inseparable.

As we sat on our cushions and waited, it was easy to see that this particular night was special. The zendo was packed, and to top it off, two monks had come in from Japan to join us. One of the monks was upstairs with us, sitting on a cushion, waiting. He looked like a willow rising from a pond.

Finally, it was seven o'clock. Bells rang, and the evening began. The monk stood up and told us he was here to give us instruction.

"This is an incredible night. It's your first time sitting in the zendo," he said so softly we could barely hear him.

Then he carefully showed us how to do zazen, and led us in our first sitting. We were to pay attention only to our breathing. Whatever we felt, whatever happened, we were to sit with our legs crossed, back straight, eyes down and not move until we heard the bell ring. He would ring the bell to start the sitting and ring it again when the sitting was over.

The bell rang out and silence descended. No one moved. Time seemed to go on and on forever. It was even harder here than at home. My knees stuck back up in the air, my back curled and my mind raced around. This couldn't be it after all those years of waiting?

Finally, the bell rang and thankfully we got up from our cushions, stood in front of them, put our palms together and bowed to each other. Then, one behind the other, in a row, we were led downstairs to the main zendo. It was now time to join those who had been sitting there.

The silence downstairs was electric. Those who had been sitting there were now walking slowly through the zendo, one behind another, eyes down. They were doing walking meditation—kinhin—paying attention to the bottom of their feet. Some were in robes, some were not. The new students joined the back of the line and followed along.

Walking through the wooden zendo, I was transported to ancient Japan. The intense silence, simplicity, fragrance and beauty were overwhelming. After the walking meditation was over, wooden clappers were struck indicating time for the second sitting.

The students who had been walking intensively in meditation stopped at their cushions and bowed to each other. Then they sat down for the second sitting. The new students were led to cushions at the end of the line and sat down as well. No one could leave until the evening was over, no matter how they felt.

A deep, resounding gong was struck to announce the beginning of the second sitting. In the deep silence that followed, new thoughts arose. Who are these people? Who am I? Why am I here? How did this happen? Along with the physical and emotional pain that came and went, thoughts arose ceaselessly. You couldn't move to get away from them either, just had to sit still until they drifted away. What were these thoughts? Where did they come from, what did they want from me?

In spite of this, the second sitting was easier. It was different sitting downstairs in the main zendo, supported by many who sat powerfully beside you without wavering.

At the end of that sitting, bells were rung again. Everyone got up, bowed and then immediately smoothed and straightened their cushions. Take care of your world and it will take care of you, I remembered reading, as I puffed out the cushion I'd sat on.

A few announcements were made about the upcoming week's schedule and we were all thanked for our attendance that night.

Then a Japanese monk at the front of the line took a few steps to the center.

"We will be serving informal tea upstairs now," he said. "If you have time, please join us. You are also all welcome at the zendo whenever you care to return."

That was it. The evening was over. I felt jarred and confused. What did all this have to do with those wonderful stories I'd been reading for years? It was too much to go to tea at the moment. I didn't want to talk, needed time to absorb this. Dazed, I walked back to my apartment, alone.

My husband, waiting at the door, couldn't wait to hear the news. "How was it? How was it?"

"It was strange, it was weird, it hurt terribly," I uttered, disconcerted.

"Really?" He was startled. "Well, you tried it, anyway," he said. "You don't have to go back."

"Of course I don't," I responded.

ॐ

I WENT TO SLEEP SAD and restless. Then, at four o'clock the next morning, suddenly, as if electrocuted, I sat bolt upright in bed. My God, my God, what happened? I couldn't wait to get back to the zendo again.

1

The Sound of the Gong

"The sound of the gong,

In the spring dawn forever."

—Soen Roshi

AFTER MY FIRST NIGHT AT the zendo, I couldn't sleep the same way again. I woke up every few hours to make sure it wasn't time to wake up, jump out of bed, and get to the zendo for early morning sitting. I couldn't bear to go through the day without the zazen there.

I'd wake up, lean across my sleeping husband and peer at the alarm clock. Two more hours to go. One more hour to go. I waited intensely to get there and hear the incredible sound of that gong. I longed for it, needed it. The day felt lonely without it.

Being at the zendo in the early morning, listening to the gong, chanting, sitting, brushed all kinds of cobwebs away. I left joyous, shot from a cannon. The sky was blue, the air smelled fresh and delicious, even in the dusty city. How come? I had no idea.

Fortunately, at that time, we lived close by. I could get there and be home before everyone got up. I'd go and return in time to make breakfast, hug the children, get the day going.

So, every morning, I'd leap out of bed at five in the morning, dress, take the elevator down to the lobby and make my way to the zendo. We lived in an apartment house near the East River, filled with couples, children, airline stewardesses and a few ladies of the night. Almost every morning, as I came down the elevator, some ladies of the night would be returning from work, coming up. These were women I never saw in the day and who never saw me. We looked at each other curiously now.

As I slipped out of the elevator one morning and one of these women was about to slip in, she stopped me.

"Tell me something, honey, where do you go every morning?" she asked, her glittery mascara streaking over her eyes. "You got us all curious. Some of us girls are even taking bets."

Should I tell her about the zendo? I wondered. Should I invite her to come, too?

"Come on, your secret's safe with me." She winked.

"I go to the zendo," I whispered, "to do Zen meditation — zazen."

She burst out laughing. "That's a good one. Tell me another." Then she stopped and stared at me. "Where's the zendo? What's zazen?" she continued quickly. "The next time the cops pick me up, I'll tell them that's where I've been. That and a hundred bucks will get me out of jail."

My heart went out to her swiftly. "Come with me to the zendo some morning," I urged more strongly. "All you need is zazen to get you out of jail."

∝ ∝

SO, MORNING AFTER MORNING I arrived at the zendo way too early and waited for the exact moment when the door would open and I could go in. The monk, the teacher I'd been waiting for, was away in Japan when I first arrived. Baijosan, another monk from Japan, had come to help for a while. He was living there then.

Baijosan was short, with a shaved head, warm heart and lively eyes He cleaned the zendo, polished the floors, put fresh flowers on the altar, cooked rice, served tea and opened the thick wooden door every morning at exactly 5:15 a.m.

At that time the early morning sitting was attended by only a few, mostly resident students, a couple of monks and a few lay students. Most had to go to work and came for evening zazen. But no matter who was or wasn't there, Baijosan appeared at the door every morning at precisely 5:15 a.m.

Most of the time when he'd peered outside, no one was to be seen. It was still dark out and the city streets were deserted. But now, whenever he came to the door, there I was, standing on the doorstep, eagerly waiting to be let in. Startled, Baijosan's eyes opened wide every time he saw me standing there in the cold.

"Come in, come in," he whispered, hurriedly. He must have

wondered why an American woman, a lay student, was so desperate to join in.

The minute he opened the door, I slipped in, pulled off my shoes, placed them in the rack and then flew upstairs to change into a new student's robe. Each morning I felt overjoyed to have arrived here, couldn't believe my fantastic luck. Once I changed and came down into the dark, freezing zendo, I put my palms together and bowed at the entrance of the meditation hall. Then I took one precise step after another along the incredibly polished wooden floor to a cushion that waited for me up front.

Once at the cushion, I bowed, sat down, crossed my legs, straightened my spine, looked down at the floor and, along with everyone else in the zendo, waited for the formal sitting to begin. Tremendous pain welled up in my legs, died down and welled up again. What was this pain? Where did it come from? I wondered. With or without an answer, I continued to sit. I sat waiting for the sound of the gong, which announced morning service was about to begin.

The moment I heard the gong, the day truly began. The gong bellowed out, welcoming me, enlivening me, reassuring me that all was well. The gong entered every pore of my body, echoing over and over, never leaving me the same again.

But despite the incredible beauty there, it was mixed, at times, with incredible pain. Our practice was to sit with it all, learn to take whatever came. This is your life, I told myself, sit through it, and see what it truly is and what it becomes.

It couldn't have been easy for anyone to have me there, either. Every day we started with morning service and I came too often, chanted too loud and cried as quietly as I could. Not quietly enough, though. My crying really troubled Baijosan. For some reason he felt tremendously sorry for me, though I had no idea why.

One morning, Baijosan finally got the courage to speak to me. It was after morning sitting. We had all gone upstairs and, still in silence, sitting on cushions on the floor, had a delicious breakfast together—fresh oatmeal and green tea. After the meal was over, I went to help wash pots in the kitchen.

Suddenly I noticed Baijosan at the sink, standing beside me, holding a dish cloth in his hand. He was looking at me intently. "Is something wrong?" he asked.

"Nothing is wrong." I was amazed that he asked.

"Why do you come every day?" he continued.

"Everything is wonderful," I replied promptly, touched by his concern.

Baijosan's nose wrinkled. He didn't buy it. "Everything is wonderful, really?"

But everything was wonderful. When I was in the zendo even the feel of the dishwater on my hands was like healing ambrosia. I had no idea how I'd ever found this place, or how it found me.

"Absolutely wonderful," I answered cheerfully. Then I wondered if something was bothering Baijosan. Was he lonely for home, was it hard to be here among Americans? "And you,

Baijosan, is everything okay?"

But Baijosan could not be diverted. "In the practice of zazen, we have to be very careful," he responded, gently.

I was happy to receive this instruction from him.

"If we're not very careful, it is not good." He waved his hands suddenly, clearing away a host of little gnats that were flying near the kitchen cabinets. "Sometimes it is better to stay home, have a good sleep, take care of your family, and not be so attached to the sound of the gong."

I shivered. How did Baijosan know how I longed for the sound of the gong?

"Take a little vacation," he suggested softly.

But there was nothing else I wanted to do, nowhere else I wanted to go. "Why?" I asked him. "Tell me."

"Because sometimes it can be dangerous to truly hear the sound of the gong."

2

Just Grab the Dust Rag

ANY MORNINGS, AFTER MORNING SERVICE and zazen, breakfast was served upstairs. Then, after breakfast, some students stayed to help with the cleaning. But mostly, after sitting, the lay students went down the street to the diner on the corner to eat breakfast together and fervently discuss what true practice was and how we could all become enlightened. And was it even possible?

It was a group of unforgettable people. Bruce was there, a brilliant musician and Chinese scholar; Min, a Korean karate master; Don, a welterweight champion prize fighter; Michael, a wonderful, lonely guy who only wanted to love. Sheila, the secretary at the zendo, stayed and made oatmeal for the monks and residents upstairs. As the group of us at the diner huddled together in our booth, we gobbled down eggs, drank coffee and talked about how we could become wise, beautiful, powerful and enlightened like the incredible monks.

In those days I had a bunch of young children and it often was hard to stay after sitting. Sometimes I could, though. I could stay not only for breakfast, but even a little longer. That was a very special day for me. Of course then I was torn between what to do. Should I use this precious time to talk about practice and start the day incredibly inspired, or should I stay at the zendo, have breakfast upstairs and then grab a dust rag and help out? Usually I decided to go to the diner and talk.

But, even as we were eating eggs and talking at the diner, there was a lot of work to do at the zendo. The altars had to be dusted, the cushions vacuumed, the wooden floors polished, and debris had to be picked up from the incredible Japanese Zen rock garden outside, in the rear. A glass door separated the outdoor rock garden from the back part of the zendo. That area was called the garden zendo and when you sat back there, it was as if the rocks were sitting with you, supporting your practice in every way.

One particular day, I decided not to go to the diner, but to stay, have breakfast upstairs, and then go down afterwards to clean. A few others also remained behind that particular day. I was assigned to dust the wood moldings all along the garden zendo and dust the altar there. Another student, Ian, from Israel, was assigned to work beside me in the garden zendo, cleaning the glass door.

Ian grabbed a rag and went right to it. He paid attention to nothing else, just cleaned so thoroughly, so intently and profoundly, that not a speck of anything was left on the glass. After the work period ended, I noticed him standing still, looking through the glass door at the beautiful, shimmering rocks. Drawn by his intensity, I immediately walked over beside him and looked as well. In the early morning light, the rocks glowed through the sparkling glass.

"You did a wonderful job," I said.

Ian just stood there transfixed. "If only I could learn to clean my house like this, it would be enough," he replied.

He said it with such wholeheartedness, it stopped me cold. That's all he wanted? That was it? Just to clean his house like this, totally? Forget about discussions with others, getting inspired, finding ultimate truth?

"That's it?" I asked him, astonished.

His radiant smile shut me up. "What else is there?" he asked sharply.

My mind started spinning. Was that what practice was about, just grabbing the dust rag, doing what was needed, doing it completely with no resistance or complaints? Was it enough to just take care of whatever popped up in front of you? Didn't this guy want something extra? What about enlightenment, becoming free, transmitting dharma, becoming a monk, opening your doors to the whole world?

"That's really all you want?" I finally asked Ian, who, at the moment, frankly scared me to death.

Ian looked at me and beamed. "What else are you looking for?"

Again, he spoke so wholeheartedly that his words rang through my life for many years. They almost became like the sound of the gong, echoing through every pore.

What was I looking for? I had no idea, but I knew for sure I had to find it. Even if it took an entire life.

3

Find Out For Yourself

E VERY TUESDAY AFTERNOON, A SITTING was scheduled. Tuesday afternoon was a good time for me, so one particular Tuesday afternoon, I went to the zendo as usual. I sat down and faced the wall, faced myself, faced the silence. There were only a few of us in the zendo that afternoon, and to my surprise, I found myself sitting on a cushion next to a Japanese monk I hadn't seen before. His powerful energy filled the space, and he sat as if rooted to the depths of the earth.

The bell rang out, zazen started and then suddenly, he spoke out. He spoke in a deep, resonant voice, punctuating the silence and startling me.

"Everyone is welcome in the zendo," he proclaimed.

It was him, I knew it! My teacher from Japan had finally arrived. I was stunned, thrilled, astonished. Every inch of my body came alive; he was here at last, was welcoming me home.

"In this practice, you are not being asked to believe anything," the monk continued, unaware of the commotion inside of me. "All you have to do is come in, sit down and find out for yourself. You must stop moving, sit like a mountain, open your eyes wide."

The moment I heard those words, I landed full square on my cushion and stayed there for the next forty years. This was the place I'd been deprived of, a place to find out for myself. All my life I'd longed to find out what really lived behind the words, lies, actions, games and dreams life threw my way. Here was a way out of madness, I thought. Of course, I didn't realize at that time that the way out of the madness was deeper into the madness—so deep that at times you didn't know who you were or where you were anymore. Or that it was even madness you were living in.

Find out for myself? Perfect, I thought. What more could anyone ask for? What had I done to deserve such a great blessing?

That afternoon was only the beginning. I sat beside him in the zendo year after year, decade after decade. As we sat together, many times I wondered what it was that brought a tough Samurai Zen monk from Japan to end up sitting next to a restless Jew from Brooklyn who sat on her cushion and cried.

"Stop crying," he would growl, as I often wept loudly, making a commotion and disturbing everyone.

I would just cry harder as, in response, his sitting grew deeper and more intense.

"Stop crying!" he would demand again.

But no matter how much he yelled and demanded silence, it took years of sitting for the crying to end. It must have been very hard for him having me there, harder than I ever realized. Now I wonder, perhaps I was crying tears he couldn't shed; perhaps the strength he had lived inside me as well.

Yet despite our radical differences, we stayed planted on the cushion beside one another for years. Of course, there were similarities as well. Both of us displaced from our cultures, both of us passionate about zazen. Years passed, shocks happened, joy, sorrow, disappointments. But no matter what, I kept returning. I had to find out for myself.

4

Nowhere to Go

"The path is made by walking on it."

—Machado

FTER SITTING IN ZAZEN THE bell rings, we rise, bow and walk in kinhin, eyes down, paying attention to the bottom of our feet. As we continue, year after year, one day we see that no two steps are like one another and that the bottom of our feet contains wisdom we haven't even begun to realize. When we take off our shoes and socks, and really feel our feet on the floor, there is no end to what we can discover.

In kinhin, we walk for about ten minutes, until clappers sound and we slowly return to our seats and bow. Where are we going when we walk? Nowhere. What will we do when we get there? Nothing. Around and around the beautiful zendo we walk, with no destination. Only the step itself matters—matters deeply. How thrilling to actually feel even one step. How shocking, how rare.

How long does it take to feel our feet on the floor? Years

maybe, lifetimes. How hard it is to focus on our feet touching the wooden floor. There are so many delicious reasons not to. All our friends in the sangha are there walking with us. It is so tempting to glance up to see who's here tonight. How are they doing? Will we meet for pizza around the corner afterwards? Occasionally, while passing one another in line, eyes meet in a furtive glance.

"Keep your eyes down!" the monitor reminds us. "Pay attention to the bottom of your feet."

But it's so tempting to look at the magnificent calligraphy of the great Zen masters that hang on the walls, to admire the exquisite flower arrangement on the altar that our monk's Japanese wife prepares for us, night after night.

"Eyes down. Pay attention! This step will not come again," our monk calls out one night, during kinhin. Someone starts to sob.

I am struck with the shock of unlived life and the incredible delicacy of time. We cannot hold onto the step and cannot let it pass, either. To truly walk, as if our life depended on it, is rare.

One day I'll do this, I tell myself. One day I'll put everything I have into the bottom of my feet as they touch the magnificent, cool, polished wooden floor. Not yet. One day! Right now too much else calls me. I miss my friends, I love seeing them. Right now, it's too much fun to look around.

When will that day come? So far it hasn't. Friends have left the kinhin line and before long my turn is coming; I've grown older now. This step, this one perfect step, will not come again.

5

Beginner's Night

O N THURSDAY NIGHTS, BEGINNER'S NIGHT, there was always a talk by a senior student. Often it was given by a gruff guy named Don Scanlon, an ex-welterweight boxing champion. Don had salt and pepper hair and a beautiful, old, beaten-up face. Whenever he talked, the air was filled with electricity. I loved listening to Don. Not only his talks, but who he was, inspired me greatly.

"I'll be giving the talk for tonight," Don said. He didn't smile, didn't have to. He was who he was, and nothing else. "Don't come here and expect to become someone special or something unusual," he continued. "There's nothing unusual about Zen. Maybe it looks like that, but don't be fooled. Come here and expect to work hard. If you're looking for miracles, don't come to Zen. The only miracle in the zendo is that you're here at all. What you end up getting here is just more of what you are. And sometimes that's not so terrific."

Everyone laughed.

"I've been sitting for about ten years now," Don went on. "And what have I learned? Just to forget about the past and stay where I am. For years I was beaten up in the ring, but it was nothing compared to what I did to myself. If there's a miracle, it's to learn how to stop beating yourself up—and everyone else. Okay, let's not waste a precious second. This is the time for zazen."

As he spoke, I felt tremendously cheerful, clear, solid, planted in my own life.

The bell rang then and we all sat together in zazen. As we sat a new student shifted on his cushion.

"Don't move," Don yelled out to him, "don't try to get away from the pain. You can't get away from it, anyway. It just comes back the next minute. Why not try something different tonight? Why not sit deep down to the root?"

Don knew what he was talking about, and the student stopped shifting immediately, straightened up and listened. The atmosphere crackled with attention. If the person who was talking at the zendo knew what they were talking about, if they'd been through it themselves, people listened. If they were just talking from books or theories, it fell flat and didn't help.

"No matter what changes or trouble life brings, Zen practice stays the same," Don continued as we sat. "You just do it over and over. You come to the zendo, sit down on the cushion, chant the same sutras and sit. You pay attention to your breath and let everything else take care of itself. Now, if that isn't fantastic, tell me what is."

People were fascinated and so was I. In those days I listened to Don for my very life. Seeing his battered face helped me; feeling his courage to stand up to all the beatings he'd gone through helped me stand up to mine. Day by day, my zazen was growing deeper and my schedule was also taking root.

The zendo was growing its roots too. More and more people were coming and returning, to practice. No matter when I went to the zendo now, there was always someone wonderful there. The place was packed with incredible students of all ages, religions, races and nationalities. They came from all walks of life, all backgrounds and life plans. Life plans or not, somehow or other, we all ended up here sitting together, wondering why.

But whether we understood why or not, there was a tremendous sense of joy at having found this place. As soon as we arrived at the zendo, we took off our masks, threw away our roles and became natural. When we walked in the door, no one looked at each other. We did not check out, judge, scan or evaluate who the person was, or who they were not. We totally abstained from that kind of violence and kept our eyes down at the floor.

When someone came to sit, if he was sad, he did not have to smile. If he was angry, he did not have to act loving. He was what he was, and no one noticed. Only he or she noticed. That was enough. How we grew to appreciate that deep form of kindness. Just allowing ourselves and one another to be exactly who and how we were.

All complications vanished. We just gathered together to sit without moving and discover who truly lived inside. We also had to discover why we were so happy together and loved each other so much.

6

A Member of the Universe

ONTHS PASSED AND I'D BECOME a regular in the early mornings. Baijosan returned to Japan, but every morning, our monk was always sitting there at the front of the row, doing such profound zazen, so profound you could feel it miles around. His zazen drew me, healed, soothed and awakened all that was waiting within. So, even though many times he scowled at me, turned away, tried to get rid of me, the very next day I would return.

Naturally, I hungered for his recognition. I wanted him to know how much I cared, how devoted I was. So, every day I arrived at five thirty in the morning and, after changing into a robe, rushed down the row to be able to sit next to him. Morning after morning, I chanted too loudly and sat with all the strength I could muster. When the pain got too great, I twisted and turned, though. He just sat there beside me, bearing this continuous irritation, not responding in any way.

In those days, after you'd been sitting for a month or so, you could become a member. I couldn't wait, counted the days excitedly. After going every day for more than two months, I finally made an appointment to see him and become a member too. It would be our first time to actually talk to each other. Nervous, after early morning zazen, I climbed the stairs to his meeting room on the second floor.

When I opened the door to his room, he was seated in zazen on a cushion on the floor, his eyes half open.

I entered and bowed.

"Come in," he said.

Overjoyed, I sat down opposite him at a low wooden table that had two teacups on it. He looked up, nodded, and very carefully, offered me a cup of delicious powdered green tea.

I received the tea and we drank together.

After we finished the tea and slowly put our cups back down on the table, he paused and looked at me.

"Yes?" he said.

"I've been sitting here for two months now," I responded, unable to contain my delight.

He looked up at me, a bit surprised. "You have?"

I was stunned. I'd been sitting right next to him for almost two months. He'd been demanding that I stop crying. How could he have not known I was there?

"Of course, I've been coming every day," I replied, "I'm here every morning." Then I stared at him, completely bewildered.

"Really?" he repeated.

"Yes," I burst out, "I've been sitting right next to you and I want to become a member now."

He looked at me sharply. "Why?"

I was speechless.

"What difference does it make, member or non-member?" he asked, somewhat scornfully.

Silence filled my heart. I hadn't stopped to consider that. Finally, I shrugged. "It makes no difference at all," I countered.

"Exactly," he said. "Interview is over."

Trembling, I hobbled back down the stairs. He never even knew I was sitting there next to him all those mornings, I thought, crushed. How was it possible he didn't even recognize me?

Later in the day my husband called me, excited. "So, congratulations, are you a member now?"

"No," I replied, defeated.

There was a long pause on the other end. My husband was as confused as I. He loved that I went to the zendo, was thrilled with the person I was turning into.

"Why not? What happened?" he asked haltingly.

Of course, once again, I didn't know.

"Did you do something to offend him?" he asked.

"Maybe I did?" I wondered.

"That's terrible," my husband replied.

"Terrible or not," I responded, "whether or not he recognizes me, I'm going to continue every day."

$\approx$ $\ll$

NOW, YEARS LATER, I SEE that the true question is not whether I did something to offend him, but why I craved recognition so. Why was it so important to become a member?

Zazen practice is not about belonging. It is not about being noticed or accepted by anyone. Even though you sit next to others, you find out what it means to be alone, to experience your aloneness through and through. As you do, you may realize that aloneness is not loneliness. In fact, it is the opposite. Zazen cuts the leaning, depending mind, makes us stand on our own two feet. The teacher's job is to take everything away, while he serves delicious green tea.

As we sit, little by little we realize that our insane desire for recognition is actually a poison that destroys our life. Addicted to approval, acceptance and adoration, many become desperate if they do not receive it. Most know themselves only through the eyes of another. Some eyes are full of adoration. Others are full of bitterness. So what? Searching for ourselves in the eyes of others, we despair. He loved me yesterday, and now he doesn't. What did I do wrong?

Nothing! Nothing! Moments change. Yesterday he was happy. Today he has indigestion. What has it got to do with you? Look at me and don't look at me are two forms of the same madness. A true Zen master wipes them both away.

☙ ❧

So, MEMBER OR NO MEMBER, I still continued going, sitting near him and doing zazen. I also continued to go upstairs with others and join them for breakfast, work and tea.

Some students were regulars, others came and went. And before long, our monk's teacher, Soen Roshi, who was the abbot of a monastery in Japan, came to join us for a while.

Soen Roshi was completely different in style, utterly playful and filled with delight. Many times when you were doing kinhin, and he was in the vestibule, as you walked by you did not even realize he was there. He seemed to blend in with the walls, with the day, with whatever he encountered.

One morning, when Soen Roshi was in New York, a few of us were upstairs in the meeting room, having tea together after zazen. It was a great thrill to be there with him, and I was nervous and excited. As I drank my tea, suddenly Soen Roshi turned and looked at me pointedly.

"Have you been here long?" he asked me kindly, his eyes sparkling.

Taken off guard, I immediately burst out, "Yes, I have. And I am not a member of the zendo yet."

He looked very surprised. "Not a member?" his deep voice echoed.

It was a perfect chance for me to tell him that I'd been coming every day, but somehow, our monk never saw me there and I was still not a member.

But instead, Soen Roshi surprised me. "Me neither," he replied, in a loud whisper, smiling.

At first I wasn't sure what he was saying.

He shook his head and repeated it. "Me, neither," he said more loudly.

I was shocked. Soen Roshi wasn't a member? How could that be?

Looking at my face he laughed. "But I am a member of the universe," he continued. "How about you? Tell me."

ॐ ॐ

HOW ABOUT ME? I COULD barely answer. I had no idea who I was these days or who I could possibly be. A member of the universe—that kind of freedom was thrilling and also very scary. I had no real idea what it meant.

But whoever I was or wasn't, when I was with Soen Roshi, I was at home. Everything was where it belonged. Whatever life brought became beautiful, intoxicating, something I could finally ease into and taste for myself.

> "Wherever I go is my home In eternity."
>
> —Soen Roshi

7

Just Freeze

INALLY, A FEW MONTHS LATER, in a very casual, offhanded way our monk allowed me to become a member of the zendo and a preparatory student. The zendo conducted both week-end and week-long retreats, or sesshins. Now I was allowed to go to my first one.

"You think you can do it?" our monk asked, upstairs in the meeting room, as we shared a cup of tea.

Not knowing what was really involved, and thrilled to be included, I nodded vigorously.

"I can do it," I said.

"I'm not sure," he challenged.

"I'll try," I uttered.

"Not enough," he exclaimed. "Either do it or don't. No trying here."

ॐ ॐ

THIS WEEKEND RETREAT THAT WAS coming up was the first sesshin for all the preparatory students, and it was to be held at the zendo. None of us had yet had dokusan with the teacher.

Dokusan was a very special interview held in the middle of intensive zazen. At this sesshin we would all go for dokusan together as a group, with our teacher, the monk.

This particular sesshin was being held during winter, and it happened to be extremely cold. Not only was there no heat in the zendo, but the doors in back leading to the Japanese garden were wide open, letting in the icy air. As all seating in the zendo was based upon seniority, preparatory students were seated in the back part of the zendo, near the open door. Unbearably cold winds blew in over us. Hopefully they were to encourage us to sit stronger and deepen our concentration. The deeper the concentration went, we were told, the less the cold would bother us. We might not even notice it was there.

It worked the opposite way for me. The longer I sat there, the colder I got. I couldn't concentrate on anything but the weather and why they refused to turn on the heat. Freezing and furious, I piled on three sweaters, and shivering, kept thinking about jumping up and closing the door. What a nut I was to sit here and take it. I dreamt of how nice it would be when I got out of here and was all warm and cozy in my home.

All of a sudden a senior student came to where we were sitting and briskly announced that the time had come. The preparatory students were to come upstairs for dokusan now!

Everyone else quickly rose and, one behind the other, rushed upstairs to the dokusan room. Totally freezing and unwilling to go anywhere, I sat right where I was.

A few minutes later, the same senior student flew back

down to where I was sitting, yanked me off the cushion, and pushed me upstairs. Horrified, I had no choice but to go.

When I entered the dokusan room it was dark. Our monk was grandly seated in his black robes in front of a single burning candle. The students were sitting, lined up in a row before him, terrified. The flame from the candle flickered wildly. No one moved. Dead silence. I was shoved onto a cushion at the end of the row.

Finally, the monk asked, "Any questions or comments?"

The silence deepened.

Suddenly, I yelled out, "It's *freezing* down there!"

"Then *freeze!*" he shouted, and rang his bell to indicate the interview was over.

Appalled, everybody got up and trailed out.

ॐ ॐ

WHEN IT IS HOT, BURN, *when it is cold, freeze.*

Although we did not know it at the time, our monk was teaching us how to escape the pain of freezing. When you are cold, freeze. When you are hot, burn. When you are sad, grieve. Whatever comes, welcome it one hundred percent, nothing left over. *Leave no traces.* Do not escape your experience. Do not avoid it in any way. This is mindfulness taken to its fullest extent, with no reservations. It is an antidote to the bondage of life which is caused by our struggle against whatever comes our way.

We are entrapped by the endless desire for things to be

different. When we let that go, when we enter a state of acceptance, the struggle against life disappears. Where is our slavery then? Then we are free to live and taste our experience completely, just as it is. At this point, suffering turns into delight and the world a place of oneness and joy. We have gone to the other shore.

ॐ ॐ

A STUDENT OF OLD SAW an old Zen grandma sitting at the side of the road, howling in pain.

"What's wrong? What happened?" he asked her.

"My grandchild has just died," she wailed.

"I thought you were enlightened. How can you be crying like this?" the student demanded.

The old woman stopped for a moment and looked at him. "How can I not?" she said.

8

Come Naked Before Me

WHEN WE WENT A LITTLE further in our practice, each of us received our own robe. Covered and sheltered in our robes, everything inessential was hidden from sight. No one could judge you by what you were wearing, nor could you judge anyone else. It didn't matter if you were fat or skinny, rich or poor. Instead of showing off your latest clothes or cut of figure, you sat, enfolded in the robe of dedication, renunciation, simplicity.

You felt it the minute you put on the robe too, a freedom surrounded you. You sat like students of old, depending upon nothing but the moment, returning to simplicity. In days of old, many practitioners only had the robe they wore and a few bowls to eat with. They renounced everything else and allowed life itself to provide.

What were these practitioners renouncing? Attachment to this fleeting world, attachment to name and form, attachment to the incredible excitement of dressing yourself up in beautiful colors and designs, hoping that others would notice what a truly exceptional, beautiful creature you were.

What were these practitioners gaining? Absolutely nothing. The gift of nothing was vast and boundless. No one could say give me more and more of it. Yet out of nothing, everything appeared. And into nothing everything disappeared.

Sadly, as time went on, our simple robes became complicated. Some received brown robes, others black, depending on rank and status. Some robes were cotton, and some robes were silk and sometimes even brocaded. These kinds of robes cost thousands of dollars and signified great success, great enlightenment, great reverence! Before long everyone was looking to see what kind of robe you had. Pride surrounded the robes, like the smell of fumes, mixing with the exquisite incense that came to us from Japan. A masquerade began. Of course this masquerade was also a great teaching, though none of us thought so. This masquerade was a reflection of life itself that we were practicing to see through.

Another Roshi, Sasaki Roshi, once said, "The whole world is a hospital, but the zendo is the intensive care unit. Take care!"

In the zendo we experienced everything more intensely, acutely. And of course, the stink of pride, an inevitable illness, also had to appear. The stink of pride can easily pollute both the practice and the practitioners. A great koan we each received was how to be free of this pollution, how to stay simple and sincere in the midst of a world where constant masquerades make us more and more tormented and blind.

൙ ൖ

BUT MASQUERADE OR NOT, IT seemed to me that whatever confusion I had, whatever appeared to disturb me, the moment I saw Soen Roshi, all difficulty melted away. Just who he was and the way he lived seemed to contain the answer to all my questions. We met on a different plane, out of form, beyond time. Yet, in our odd meetings we became good friends. And, even better than that—real friends forever.

To my delight, Soen Roshi began coming more and more frequently to join us. It seemed to me that Soen Roshi was never caught by the masquerade. When he looked at us, he did not look with external eyes. He saw the depth of beauty in us all and became one with each and every person.

During sesshin, we could go to Soen Roshi for dokusan. Whenever I came to see him, I felt he was so happy to see me. And I was so happy to see him, too.

"Come before me naked," Soen Roshi would say, then his eyes would twinkle, and he'd wait for a reply.

I always shivered.

"When?" he asked, his voice rising like a bell from the bottom of the earth.

"I'm trying," I answered feebly, at first.

His face puckered. "Nothing to try. Naked is naked."

Of course, he didn't mean to rip off my robes. He didn't care about my body. He meant to let go of attachment to everything that was not real, of the longing to be somebody else.

But I couldn't do it, and Soen Roshi saw my confusion, how

complicated my life had become.

"Let's play," he offered, and would get down on the floor and play with me, like two little children together.

It was so much fun, I laughed and laughed in a way that I hadn't my entire life. Of course he had no idea that I'd never had a chance to play like that and sorely needed it. He had no idea but still, he knew, and followed his inner knowing completely.

"We're playmates," he said, over and over, "let's just have wonderful time."

Despite the pain, despite the struggle and disappointments, since then my zazen practice has always been about playing, giving myself and others a great gift and having a wonderful time.

જ ન્ક

SOEN ROSHI'S TEACHINGS WERE A form of play itself. One time we were all expecting him to arrive from Japan to join us in a weekend sitting. Our monk became even more diligent to make the zendo and its students perfect for the occasion. Great preparations went on, the floors polished extra brightly, each cushion vacuumed with extra care. The flower arrangement was larger and more beautiful, and every moment of the welcome service for Soen Roshi was choreographed and planned. I saw how excited our monk was to receive his teacher and show him how beautifully the zendo was growing. Perhaps our monk, too, wanted recognition and acclaim. Why shouldn't he? I thought.

The day arrived. The zendo was packed. The energy and excitement was high as we sat extra strongly, awaiting Soen Roshi's imminent arrival. Any moment now he would walk through the door. We waited and waited.

He didn't come.

Distraught, distressed and deeply embarrassed, our monk said a few words to us, and then directed us to continue the schedule as if nothing unusual had taken place.

But, of course, something unusual had taken place. Something disappointing, distressing, confusing, upsetting. But it was a great teaching Soen Roshi was offering, as well. Do each thing for itself only—*moshotoku.* Do it one hundred percent without depending on the outcome. If you polish the floors, polish them thoroughly, but not for recognition or thanks. Take each moment as it comes and let go of the endless expectations that impede the natural flow. And mostly, mostly, don't depend on others!

And most poignantly, Soen's teaching was a reminder not to be attached to form. *Form is emptiness, emptiness is form,* we recited again and again. We had to be ready. One day, Soen Roshi, as we knew him, would not return again.

☙ ❧

SOEN ROSHI CAME AND WENT, but the main teacher at the zendo was our monk. Soen Roshi and our monk were very different. Our monk was fierce, strong, demanding dedication in practice. He demanded it from himself as well. He never missed a sitting with us, was always upstairs after morning zazen, available to handle whatever came along. He was always where he said he would be. No detail in the zendo was overlooked. Time mattered to him deeply. Even though it was a great teaching, Soen Roshi's not coming was a blow to him.

9

No Graduation

WHETHER OR NOT SOEN ROSHI was there, the schedule continued, month in and month out. Without fail, there were spring and winter training periods.

"Here we are, at the beginning of a new training period," our monk proudly announced one spring evening. "We gather together, sit on the cushion, do zazen. When the bell rings we stand up. We bow to each other and walk in kinhin. When the clappers hit we bow, walk back to our cushions. We do the same thing over and over again, year after year, nothing else, nothing special. There is no beginning and no ending, no graduation for any of us."

Then the wooden clappers were struck, the gong sounded and the lights dimmed.

"Nowhere to go," he reminded us, "nowhere to run away from."

A deeper silence descended over the zendo. All of us together, sitting as one.

This night our monk kept speaking as we sat. "Don't ask why you are doing this. Don't ask anything. Don't look for results. Don't think that one day it will be over."

I took a deep swift breath and let it out slowly.

"Nothing is ever over and nothing begins. Realize that and all is done."

The sitting went on for two hours, with one short break for walking in between. When it was over, I went out into the vestibule to put on my shoes.

"I heard that talk before," a Zen friend said to me as we were kneeling together, tying our shoes. "In fact, I've heard it at least three other times."

"Why should this training period be any different?" I asked. "What are you hoping for?"

৵ ৶

IT IS THE ENDLESS CRAVING for something more, the desire to use each moment as a means to get somewhere, that steals our precious life away. We never taste what is here right before us, we never experience the exquisite pleasure of allowing striving to subside completely. And to finally be satisfied and whole.

And, what is better than the fullness of the moment? What more do we really have?

> *"The path continues*
> *endlessly,*
> *Spring mountain."*
>
> —Soen Roshi

10

Where Are You From?

STUDENTS CAME AND STUDENTS LEFT, but stubbornly, I continued. As our monk saw me persisting, he must have decided to intensify my practice. One morning, after zazen, I was specifically invited to go upstairs and have breakfast with him and a few students.

Sheila, a beautiful, gentle resident at the zendo, tapped my shoulder lightly. "Please join us," she said. Then she smiled brightly. "I'm so glad you're with us," she whispered.

I was so glad to know her too. She was a gentle balm of kindness to all.

Upstairs, we all sat silently on the floor around a long wooden table, unpacked little eating bowls and filled them with a breakfast of oatmeal, peanuts and warm milk. After eating in silence, we washed our bowls and wrapped them up again. Then all got up and went together into the meeting room to sit in a circle on the floor with our monk and have a cup of tea.

That morning, our monk suddenly turned to me directly, as I was sipping my green tea. "And where are you from?" he asked sharply.

All eyes turned to me. At first I wanted to say from Brooklyn, but instead, I just looked up at him and smiled. He smiled back for a moment. In that split moment we recognized each other; compatriots, warriors, ancient companions. And in that moment, I realized that he would not make it easy for me, he could not, did not dare. For a sword to grow strong and worthy, it has to be tested in many fires.

"Where are you from?" he asked more pointedly.

"Nowhere at all," I replied.

He made a funny face. "Really?" Everyone laughed; I laughed too.

"Where are you from?" he boomed more loudly then, an edge of anger in his tone.

"Here."

"Where?"

"Here."

"You must sit more," he said rather kindly then. "It's imperative!"

"I will."

"Good."

Then Sheila poured us all another cup of tea.

"Do your best," our monk demanded, "your very best."

I'm trying, I whispered to myself. Believe me, I'm learning what it means to really try.

❧ ❧

TO MY DISMAY, THE QUESTION of where I was from intensified. Suddenly I had to move with my family out to Long Island,

and felt bereft of being so close to the zendo every day. Many mornings, in all kinds of weather, I would wake up at four o'clock and get on the Long Island Expressway to race to the zendo in time for morning service. Something was deeply missing if I didn't hear the sound of the gong.

One day as I came huffing and puffing into the dressing room, a senior student, Nora Seisen, was rattled. "What's wrong with you?" she said in a sharp tone. "You race here like a lunatic in the dark, at sixty miles an hour, just to stop and sit quietly. It's nuts. What's your problem?"

What was my problem? I didn't really know, but was determined to solve it anyhow.

Running after something we can't find, solving problems that do not exist and making endless mistakes, is part of this precious practice. Waking up from it for a few moments is also part of the way. Whatever life brings is practice, I began to realize, whether I liked it or not. The question was how did I greet it? Did I breathe it in and breathe it out, or did I struggle to change it, fight, judge and wipe it out?

The more I grabbed the dust rag, did what was in front of me to do, the more wholehearted I was about it, the more I was brought face to face with what I was doing and able to move on.

"*Samsara is Nirvana*," our monk proclaimed. He was saying that life as we know it is perfection. There's nothing to escape or run away from. I thought of that frequently as I dashed blindly along the highway in my car. How could I become totally peaceful with everything? Was it by sitting in endless zazen?

At first I thought so, but no matter how much I rushed to the zendo, sat, cleaned, and chanted, no matter how wonderful I felt that day, the next day, something else happened. I had to start all over again. How could I remain in uninterrupted happiness? How could I become imperturbable amidst endless change?

Whenever that question came upon me, I could not help but remember what our monk told our group in our first interview.

"When you're cold, freeze!"

When you're hot, sweat! When you're sad, be sad, one hundred percent. Take what comes, experience it completely, and forget about figuring it out.

Rinzai, a very great Zen teacher, said this in his own way.

> *"When I'm hungry, I eat,*
> *When I'm tired, I sleep.*
> *Fools laugh at me,*
> *But the wise understand."*

How many of us can actually follow this very simple direction? How many even know when they're hungry? We eat when we're sad or tired or to be social with friends. Usually, we eat too much or too little. We starve ourselves to look thin. We binge for pleasure, or distraction. When we're tired, we drink coffee to keep us going. We push ourselves beyond measure. To be aware of and respond to the natural flow of our true needs and desires is so simple, and yet so difficult.

11

"Bad Karma Relations, Good Dharma Relations"

—Soen Roshi

A FEW WEEKS LATER SOEN Roshi came for one of his visits. I was sitting in the zendo, it was early morning and out of nowhere, he ran up behind me and whispered in my ear.

"Bad karma relations, good dharma relations."

I was stunned. What made him say that? How did he know I was tossing and turning inside? My mind stopped spinning for a while as I realized that he was saying that all the difficulty I'd gone through, all the struggle and pain that was taking place now, was actually a gift, if used properly. The words went deep inside. The pain and confusion was good for my practice of dharma. It forced me to sit, it forced me to grow.

I placed my palms together in gassho, offering thanks.

"Do not avoid bitterness," he continued, whispering more intensely.

I won't, I thought to myself, and, once again, bowed.

"Okay? Okay?" he kept whispering.

"Okay." I nodded, having no idea what I was saying okay to.

ॐ ॐ

NOT AVOIDING BITTERNESS IS EASIER said than done. Normally, when we are hurt or insulted, we feel justified in lashing back. We think the person's behavior gives us the right to do so. However, in Zen practice, no matter what happens, we learn to remain firmly planted in our center and fully be with whatever is going on. Then whatever response we make will not be a knee-jerk reaction, but appropriate and healing to the occasion. It will come from a deeper part of ourselves.

Zen practice teaches that whatever happens arises from seeds we have planted at one time or another. Difficult times have been created by thoughts, deeds, desires and feelings that have been habitual in our lives (and past lives as well). When these run automatically, they inevitably create consequences. What we sow, we shall reap. If we have dwelled upon thoughts and deeds of anger, negative situations return in response.

Actually, difficult karma, a turbulent, painful inner and outer life, can actually become a blessing when it becomes fuel for practice. When we choose to turn our suffering around, our karma lessens and alters as well. We do not fuel hatred in the world, but become a source of peace.

A teaching recited at morning service describes this perfectly:

"If by any chance a friend should turn against us
And become a sworn enemy,
And abuse and persecute us,
We should sincerely bow down with humble language
In the reverent belief that he is
The merciful avatar of Buddha
Who uses devices to emancipate us
From sinful Karma
That has been produced and accumulated
Upon ourselves
By our own egoistic delusions
Through the countless cycles of kalpa."

—from The Bodhisattva's Vow

འ ༄

THAT MORNING, AFTER ZAZEN WITH Soen Roshi, I went upstairs for breakfast and tea. We all ate silently, did our work, and I was about to leave when Soen Roshi called for me.

Gratefully, I ran to talk to him.

"Eshin, if you sit only eight hours a day, every day, all your confusion will vanish," he said.

"Eight hours a day?"

"Then every newspaper you read will turn into a Sutra," he went on. "Okay?"

"Okay," I said. Okay, I get it, I thought, having no idea how I could actually do this. Firstly, I had four small children I was raising. How in the world could I do zazen eight hours a day?

Having lived for years on a mountain, doing hermit practice before he became the Abbott of Ryutakaji, Soen Roshi had no idea of what raising four little children was like, I thought. That was my first excuse. Confusion rising like mist from a flame.

The second excuse was shared by everybody—shared confusion we might say. Eight hours a day for Soen Roshi is nothing, everyone agreed. That's monk's practice he's talking about. But the Buddha dharma is being transmitted here to the West, though, now, to lay students. It's being plucked out of the monasteries and planted in everyday life. Who can sit eight hours a day anymore? Who knows if they even need to? Sitting eight hours a day could even possibly drive you crazy.

I liked that excuse better. It made sense, took me off the hook. I also knew it was all wrong. Of course it could be done, if I really, truly wanted to. After all, I had twenty-four hours a day to live in. How many of those hours rolled by in a fog? How many were lived to the fullest? How many days turned into a Sutra before my eyes?

The next time I saw one of my dear dharma brothers, Vinny, I told him what Soen Roshi said.

Vinny loved Soen Roshi. Vinny was one of the very first residents up at the monastery and lived in the little house near the lake even when it was very cold. He cleaned it up, kept it warm and did zazen a lot, alone, even when Soen wasn't there.

"It's a great idea," Vinny said, "let's try it. At least one day a week to start."

So, one day a week, on Wednesdays, Vinny came to my

home on Long Island, where I made a beautiful place to sit up on the second floor of the garage. It was all wood, with huge beams, sloping ceilings and incredible light that shone in through a tiny window.

We climbed up to the zendo at seven a.m. on Wednesday mornings, after I made breakfast for the children, and had a helper get them to school that day. Then we did zazen together until three in the afternoon, when the kids came home from school, running up the driveway, wondering where their mother had gone. The day flew by like silk and dew as we sat, walked and drank delicious green tea.

When I crawled back down from the garage when we finished, each child looked like a magnificent gift, glowing with beauty. How come?

Doing zazen for eight hours on Wednesday wasn't really hard at all, I realized. In fact, if I really wanted to, I could get up earlier each morning, do a few hours before everyone woke. I could do that again, midafternoon, and certainly later into the night. I was young then and had huge energy. Now as the years have passed I realize I never did it, though. And where did that precious energy go?

"I am joining
In your meeting
With One Mind."

—Soen Roshi

12

Don't Waste This Precious Life

"The Unexamined Life Is Not Worth Living"

IT WAS EASY TO BECOME complacent or discouraged sitting on the cushion, year after year. The greatest need all of us had was for encouragement. Our monk was a true master at keeping the flames stoked, not letting us fall back to sleep.

"Until you've found it you haven't lived," he yelled fiercely in the zendo one night. "Then what are you? Only ghosts and weaklings, haunting trees and woods. You're fools haunting valleys and streams."

There weren't too many valleys or streams in mid-Manhattan, yet I knew he was onto something. And the way he spoke, I was spellbound, his voice so deep, his eyes so piercing. Even though he had warned us not to believe a word he said, but to come to the zendo and find out for ourselves, he mesmerized me. I sat drinking in word after word.

But it wasn't a simple matter with him, either. You never knew what to expect. He could be unbearably gentle, kind and loving. At those times he would relish each one of us totally, marveling at every form of life's manifestation. A naturally great actor, he'd transport us with Japanese poetry and proclaim the teachings of the old masters as if they were happening this very moment.

Then, suddenly, thunder clouds swirled and he became aflame with the intensity of teachings that lived inside him. They roared out of him as a primal flame, demanding total commitment.

I wasn't the only one captivated. Many brilliant, wonderful students came to the zendo. They all loved what our monk said, they all loved him and sat entranced and resonated. He spoke with such profound strength, warmth and humor that even the wooden beams swayed as he grandly proclaimed the dharma—the truth of life—the essential reality! Not only the wooden beams swayed; the students also shivered.

"Don't waste a minute! Find it *now!*" our monk demanded again and again, encouraging us to sit stronger and stronger.

Of course no one ever hinted that there was absolutely nothing to find, that everything we ever needed was right here in front of our eyes. And always would be—always!

"If you believe what I say you're a fool," he chided us then. He loved and adored chiding us. It seemed to satisfy a deep need that drove him from Japan to America, a land he lovingly referred to as filled with barbarians. "If you don't sit and find out for yourself, you're a fool, a madman, not worthy of my wasting my stick on you. Your precious life will be wasted. Entirely wasted!"

My God, what could be worse than a life entirely wasted? It was my deepest hidden fear. All around me I'd seen lives wasted, tossed up on the rocks of regret, fantasy and loss. But here in this exquisite zendo I felt there was a chance not to waste this precious life. Did I have to sit eight hours a day, though? I wasn't really sure.

Of course in this practice you couldn't figure anything out because the practice itself forbid it. As we sat, we stopped dwelling in the mad, twirling mind. We also lost our faith in the power of logic, and that which seemed reasonable.

"Life is not rational, life is not reasonable," our monk proclaimed time and again.

I could certainly relate to that. And beyond that, Zen practice taught us how not to get caught in the endless mixed messages we received daily, both in the zendo and in our lives. So it seemed quite natural for our teacher and the instructions we received to contradict themselves. We had to get beyond all that. Over and over we heard:

"Be smart and be a fool. Be strong and like a willow. Stay determined and empty out. Be powerful and be no one. Listen to what I say, and forget everything you've ever learned."

I knew, of course, that contradictions, mixed messages and paradoxes were the heart of Zen practice, but where did that leave me? Totally confused.

I finally told our monk how I felt.

"Confusion is wonderful," he grandly exclaimed. "Finally, you're making progress. The ground under your feet is shaking."

True, the ground beneath my feet was both shaking and

more solid at the same time.

A little later, when Soen Roshi was in New York, I told him the same thing. "I'm confused," I complained.

"Do not be confused by your confusion." Soen Roshi smiled. "Confusion is only confusion. It doesn't mean a thing. Keep sitting, keep sitting. And one day all your beautiful confusion will melt like snowflakes on a windowpane."

And it was so. For a few precious moments confusion melted. Only to reappear again in a new form. Why wouldn't it? What kind of dream was I cooking up now?

ॐ ॐ

TIME WENT BY, AND THOUGH Soen Roshi came and went, it was our monk who I sat beside, listened to daily, grappled with from the bottom of my soul. He was hard for me and I was hard for him. Whatever I did seemed to irritate him. Whatever he did began to irritate me as well. Mostly, he was formal and strict. I was informal and lively. He wanted more dedication from me. Students were becoming ordained, becoming monks and nuns. I saw it all around me, but could not take that route. Originally, I did not see this as a religion, but as a life practice, for all. Not only did I have a family, I was dedicated to my Jewish heritage. I saw zazen as a way to deepen and illuminate that as well.

"I cannot take Buddhist precepts," I told our monk definitively, one day.

He understood completely. "Do not if you feel the least pressure," he agreed. "But do sit more, this precious opportunity may not come again." More than anything he wanted to encourage us all. About that, he was unconditional.

I heard what he said, but not deeply enough. I thought time lasted forever.

Finally, one evening, exasperated, he made another effort. It was during tea, after evening sitting. The whole sangha was upstairs in the dharma hall, all sitting in a circle, drinking tea and talking to each other. It was a moment of relief and enjoyment and I was chatting with others, smiling.

Of course he never much liked to see me smiling, relaxing or wasting my precious time when the great matter of life and death had not yet been settled. That evening, as I lifted my teacup, in front of all others, he suddenly roared at me.

"You're wasting time, wasting time. Do not be deceived by others!"

Stunned, I shook from head to toe, as if struck by lightning. But this time I growled back. "I'm already deceived, I was born deceived. I'll die deceived. Deceived forever!"

He sneered as he rose from his cushion and strutted out, muttering, "Wasting your precious time—wasting."

And, of course, I was wasting his precious time, too. How I regret it now, how I regret it, thrown up upon the rocks of regret.

> *"Phantasm and phantasm*
> *Walk together*
> *Summer begins."*
>
> —Soen Roshi

13

I Can't Stay and I Can't Go

ONCE AGAIN SOEN ROSHI VISITED from Japan. This time he came with a mission, something important to do. During that visit our monk was made into a Zen master, a Roshi. And my name was changed to Eshin. New parts of ourselves were being born.

"'Eshin' means wisdom and faith," the Roshi said. "A name to grow into. It could take hundreds of years. Or, if you're diligent, it could happen just like that!"

What could happen? Everyone here had the constant feeling that anything could happen, everything was possible. And it was. But still, questions haunted me. As zazen deepened, I could not avoid the persistent questions that rose up within.

"During zazen," our Roshi said in a talk, "everything that is within comes up to be seen. It comes up to be digested. This does not happen consciously, but it happens nevertheless. Be very careful. Do not get caught."

Intense memories were arising, though, that touched my heart, bringing inexpressible sadness about my entire family, cousins, parents, sister, brother, all of them. Am I abandoning you? I wondered. I flinched, became restless and suddenly started to stand up.

"Sit down, Eshin," the Roshi insisted. "Wait for the bell to ring out."

I sat back down and memories of the past came more insistently. What am I really doing here? I wondered. Am I involved in idol worship? I shuddered.

In the beginning of my practice of zazen, I did not worry about idol worship. I didn't worry about anything. Soen Roshi said over and over that Zen was a practice, not a religion, and I just returned to the beautiful wooden zendo and sat there every day. Now, things were changing. He was not here often, and I was face to face with our monk who was now the Roshi.

One day I went to speak with him about it directly. "I was raised as a Jew," I started.

He listened silently and respectfully. "I understand."

"Idol worship, I'm afraid of it," I continued.

"The Buddha statue is not an idol." His answer was sharp and quick. "It is a reminder of balanced mind and body."

I could not help but remember the words of my childhood training, warning us not to get lost on strange pathways. Do not worship false Gods, or there would be a terrible price to pay.

"False Gods," I murmured.

"We do not worship anything here, Eshin," the Roshi insisted. "We wake up to the truth of our lives and ourselves."

It didn't help to hear that. That could also be a false God,

worshipping ourselves or our teachers, I thought. My confusion and pain redoubled.

"You do not have to do anything here you're not comforta-
ble with," the Roshi replied, kindly.

That was something, but it wasn't enough.

Of course he saw my trouble. He also saw that he could do
nothing about it.

"We are karma beings," he said, trying once more to help.
"Just sit more, Eshin. Your zazen will melt this torment away."

I tried. Months went by, but nothing lasts; how could it?
The time of intense practice and concentration, the beauty,
clarity and silence I had found, was becoming endangered.
Seriously endangered. But danger was fine. Real practice
included everything, times of great calm and turbulence too.
We couldn't have one without the other. Practice came in every
way.

"Sit," the Roshi kept urging me. "Eshin, sit. Do zazen."

But now it became harder to hear him. "Roshi, I feel I
should go home."

"Where is your true home?" he tried again.

I breathed deeply for a moment.

"Your true home. Before you were born. Eshin, calm down.
You have not done wrong. You are not doing wrong here."

"According to my people I should not be here."

"Then leave."

"I can't."

"Then sit more deeply, to the very bottom of the well. Finally, when you are ripe, you will see that we are all One."

Sesshin

(Intensive Practice Periods)

14

Going to Sesshin

SESSHIN IS AN INTENSIVE TRAINING period, usually seven days, where we leave our lives behind and commit to practice from early morning until late at night. The day begins at four or five a.m. and ends at nine or ten at night. Sometimes later. Each participant is required to keep the schedule, no matter how he or she feels. Most of the day and night consists of periods of zazen with short times for kinhin. There are cleaning periods and a rest period, along with time for taking delicious vegetarian meals in zazen posture. There is no speaking the entire time, except at the interviews with the Roshi.

This is a time to collect our scattered energies and go deeper into our practice and our lives. We go beyond what we think we are capable of, confront obstacles and difficulties and simply march on. The bell rings, you get up, put one foot in front of another and walk. The bell rings again, and you return to your cushion and sit down.

During sesshin everything is more intense, including the talks the Roshi gives. He exhorts us not to waste this precious opportunity, to practice with all our strength.

As the days go by, zazen grows deeper. Times of great pain and great joy arise. We learn where our pain comes from, how to be with it without moving or disturbing others. Then we notice how the pain subsides. Where did it come from? Where does it go?

After a seven-day sesshin, you do not return home the same person. Something is forever altered; new space is made in your life stream.

15

Stop Crying

IT WAS EVENING OF THE third day of sesshin. We'd been sitting in zazen for seventeen hours a day up at the monastery. By now the pain was almost unbearable and I was exhausted as well. I wanted to go home. My legs were aching and my back was stiff. I couldn't stand the thought of sitting for another second, but it was time for the evening period to begin. People were filing in and sitting down on their cushions. They all looked fine. What was wrong with me? Three more hours to go. I didn't think I could make it.

I sat down on my cushion and listened to the bells ring out. After the bells, absolute silence. Soon the pain began to mount. There was no way I could escape it. The more I fought it, the worse it became. Beside myself, I broke the silence and started sobbing. I knew I was disturbing others, but I couldn't stop. The more I cried, the worse I felt.

Then, to my horror, Don, the head monk, shouted at me loudly, "Eshin, shut up or get out. If you don't stop crying, you'll have to go sit by yourself down at the lake. There is no pain. You are the pain. Become stronger than the pain."

At that moment I stopped struggling. The pain went. I went. Instead, there was incredible joy.

Sesshin is a great medicine for sorrow. As you sit you see that sorrow and joy are simply two sides of one hand. You no longer give either of them the ability to derail your life. When you live in this manner, compassion develops toward everything you encounter and your actions naturally bring benefit and avoid harm.

This evening, elated that the pain had disappeared, I ran to the Roshi in dokusan and told him the news.

"I sat through the pain, the pain vanished. I crossed the river. I went beyond."

He made a very sour face at me then. "Beyond what? Beyond where? March on, Eshin.

March on."

March on. Keep going on. That was his mantra. I obeyed.

March on to where? It didn't matter, no one knew, just march on. The greatest sin, the greatest terror, was not to march ON! In fact, every March there was a March On Sesshin—a time of renewal and marching on.

16

I Want Another Seat

URING SESSHIN THE SEATING IN the zendo was arranged according to seniority, so you always ended up sitting next to the people you started practicing with. One way or another, Sara and I were always seated next to each other. We'd started at the zendo the same night, but never really liked each other. I found her hard to take and she couldn't stand me.

Once, on our way up to a sesshin at the monastery the irritation between us in the car was particularly great. When we got out, she tried her best to calm things down. As we stood outside under the vast sky, she placed her palms together and bowed to me.

"I bow to the Buddha within you," she said.

I thought it was pretentious and didn't like it.

She realized that her gesture had no effect. At this point, it was too much for her. She truly didn't want to spend another seven days sitting on the cushion next to me again. Sara decided to take matters into her own hands.

As soon as she got inside, I watched Sara talk to the senior student who had arranged the seating.

"I want another seat," she begged, "anywhere, it doesn't matter. I want another neighbor. I can't stand sitting next to her one more minute."

I actually felt the same way.

Sara pleaded and pleaded, but nothing could be done. Here we had to face whatever life brought us. Our particular likes and dislikes meant nothing. Everyone wants a perfect neighbor; how many of us have one, though?

Once again, she and I ended up beside one another on the cushion for a full week. As we both went to many sesshins, we had to live through the long hours and years of sitting side by side, confronting our aggravation. We were doomed to be stuck with each other forever, I thought.

Finally, Sara took time off to deal with personal matters. I was so relieved. Then, unexpectedly, several months later, I was having lunch in an out of the way restaurant downtown, and she walked in. We were both completely startled to see one another and ran to greet each other with great joy. It was as if I were greeting a long-lost sister. I had no idea how much I'd missed her.

"Here you are." She hugged me, delighted. "I'd felt part of me was gone."

From that time on, we were the best of friends, and I was with her during many life situations that arose. Despite the initial friction between us, our Buddha nature, our compassion and ability to accept reality, had grown. When it was strong enough, the irritations of the past dissolved into the sun.

Then, from out of nowhere came Sara's surprising illness and sudden death. As she was dying, she thanked me for being her sitting partner all these years and asked me to help with funeral arrangements. Before I knew it, I stood at the burial grounds at the monastery where we had practiced together all these years. Where was she now? I wondered. How could I possibly go to sesshin without her being there?

I stood alongside of the Roshi, monks and nuns, friends, and Sara's children and family, who brought her ashes to be interred.

The Roshi chanted powerfully as the early summer sun slanted through the trees, making odd shadows on the ground. What were all of those years of struggle between us? I wondered as I watched her ashes being placed in the soil.

After the service, tea and cookies were served in the small house near the lake. The Roshi joined in, and at one point, turned to me and said, "Eshin, you are a good friend." I never forgot that. It was one of the only times he ever praised me. And it was enough. To be a good friend was everything. In fact, to this day, many years later, I still feel Sara, at times, sitting beside me on the cushion, lending support and encouragement, a good friend as well.

17

An Escape Artist

NEEDLESS TO SAY, AS SESSHIN progresses and we sit through long hours often filled with difficulty, everyone wants to run away. And I did, over and over. I couldn't help it. When sesshin started at first I was tremendously excited, sat with great determination, and then boom—time to go. I couldn't stay another second, ran away. Sometimes I left during the night, other times in the late afternoon.

But the rules of sesshin were inviolable. They were there to help us pass through difficult times such as these. Naturally, when energy flags, discouragement arises and hopelessness stares in your face, just as in life, you want to flee. Sesshin schedule is a guard against this. You are not permitted to leave or to miss one sitting. The schedule insists that you keep practicing throughout different moods and moments, learn how to be with them all. You never know when things will change either. One sitting you may be in hell, the very next one, in the middle of heaven.

Whether in hell or heaven doesn't matter; when the times

comes for sitting, we sit. We get up when the bell rings, walk one behind another in kinhin, feeling our feet on the polished wooden floor. Then when the bell rings again, we go back and sit down on our cushion and start all over again. Suddenly, the very next sitting, a breakthrough can happen. The discouragement can melt, clarity can come. Our view of life can shift in a second. From being caught in a stuck place, in a confine of darkness, the sky opens and we can see our lives from a wide vista, filled with possibilities and joy. Then, of course, the very next sitting this can all change again. Like life itself, we never know what's coming. But we do learn how to be with whatever comes. We sit with it. We feel it, taste it, experience it, one hundred percent.

Sometimes the difficulty, or good feelings, can go on for hours, for days, even for months. Eventually, our attention refocuses. We don't care so much about what we are feeling, we just care about what we are doing right now.

But, even so, as we practice, the longing to escape can become intense. There are many ways in which we escape. We escape by sleeping, daydreaming, remembering, planning. Anything not to be with what's going on right now. During times of great boredom, memories of wonderful events from our life can keep us entertained. Fantasies rise up from nowhere and claim our attention and our lives, old grudges and vendettas haunt us. Sometimes all of this stops and we get a glimpse of how addicted we are to entertainment and drama, how our entire lives easily become one distraction after the next.

Despite the strong rules of sesshins and my teacher's un-flagging encouragement, at a certain point, I always seemed to have had enough. Sometimes I was able to sit through and arrived at the end of sesshin. Then I felt totally joyous, victorious, shocked. Many times I could not.

This is crazy, it's nuts, I began to think when it was hard to stay. The sittings are too long, the bells are too loud, the weather's too cloudy. The person next to me is breathing too hard. If I had the right partner next to me on the cushion, then things would be different. Then I could endure. Anything to excuse the horrible restlessness that arose within.

Pictures of home also kept arising endlessly. When they became too persistent, I began to plan my escape. I would slip out the back door of the monastery, load up my car and drive away after the last bell. But where did I escape to? Where?

Driving happily home in my little red car, windows open, legs stretched out, radio playing my favorite songs, I was thrilled at first that I did it! I got out of there. As I drove down the long, winding, bumpy road that led from the monastery to the main highway, there was an initial sense of elation and freedom. Whew, free at last. This is it. I'm finished. There was no way I was returning again.

Once back on the highway, I'd pull up at a diner, get hot coffee and the biggest piece of chocolate cake I could find. Chocolate cake never, ever tasted so wonderful. I'd linger on every bite and decide that this time was truly the end. There was no way I was ever going back. For over thirty years, every time I left, I thought it was the end.

Finally, when things settled down, after sesshin was over, I'd simply return to the zendo as usual. The Roshi never once said one word to me about it. It was strange to me, but I'd come back and we'd start all over again.

When They Come, We Welcome, When They Go, We Do Not Pursue is a famous Zen saying. The Roshi lived this with me over and over again. Maybe he knew that wherever I ran, the unanswered koan would keep dragging me back. Maybe he was relieved that I was gone. But it didn't matter. As I kept practicing, old fictions about life and myself departed. Slowly, I became quieter and emptier than before. My false, fantasizing mind was fading.

One time it was different. After I'd made my escape from sesshin and pulled up at my favorite diner, got my coffee, bit into my chocolate cake, I suddenly realized there was no place to run to. Where was I going, anyway?

Horrified, I got up, paid for my cake, left the diner, and turned my little red car around back up to the monastery.

When I walked into dokusan later that evening, I just sat before him and smiled. He looked at me undaunted.

"Coming and going lead nowhere," he said softly.

I nodded.

He smiled. We both knew.

"March on now," he said quietly.

I'd felt as if I'd passed a koan, walked through a closed

door. But that was not the end of the story, or of practice. It was actually the beginning. Now zazen went deeper. Now I had to sit more, not less. Old problems, sorrows, questions still came up in many ways, it's just that I held them differently.

Of course, there was more to do, more koans to grapple with. I was even given the old ones I thought I'd passed and failed them completely once again. The biggest difference is that I was no longer so much at war with what went on. I wasn't trying to figure the odds so much, hoping for success and approval, or searching for some ultimate answer that would miraculously stop all my pain. If it rains, I let it rain. If it didn't, I'd walk in the sun.

> *"Looking for serenity*
> *You have come to the mountain,*
> *Looking for serenity*
> *I am leaving*
> *The monastery.*
> *Kwatz!*
> *Stop running about seeking.*
> *The dusty affairs of the world*
> *Fill the day,*
> *Fill the night."*
>
> —Soen Roshi

18

Nine Generations of Your Family Will Be Healed

"THERE ARE MANY PITFALLS IN the practice of Zen," the Roshi said at a talk during Sesshin. "It is easy to become confused and fall. But a good student learns how to get up quickly again."

I sat straighter.

"The universe as we know it is not the way it appears to be. It is a flash of lightning, a dew drop only. Thus it is to be regarded. Do you understand?"

Although we all thought we understood, nobody did.

He continued anyway. "It does not matter what you do or do not understand, just keep working with your koan. Once you become fully enlightened, then not only you but nine generations of your family will become free."

Nine generations of my family? I could hardly suppress the joy that rose. A sudden picture of my grandmother Devorah popped into my mind. I saw her with her big wig on, her body covered, endlessly moving about in her white-tiled kitchen. I heard the words she always said under her breath, "Who is left to help the world? Where can you find a real Tzaddik [sage]?"

I looked over at the Roshi. Grandma, I longed to whisper to her, could it be possible that I found him? Would you ever want to meet my Roshi?

But once again, the Roshi's voice interrupted the reveries that went on endlessly within. "Perhaps it might seem like a strange thing to talk about the generations of our families and about death on this beautiful spring afternoon, when new life is about to bloom. But please remember, there is no spring without winter, no life without death. One generation passes so another can come. We, too, must die to the old to allow the new to be born. Without the cold death of winter, how can the spring come?"

I thought of the spring back in Borough Park, Brooklyn, of the few bluebells that struggled for air, and of the garden my grandmother always planted full of purple and yellow irises.

"If you do not understand, that is well and good," the Roshi continued. "Do not try to understand. Sit with whatever is said as if it were a koan."

I breathed a little more easily then.

What is a koan? Specifically, a koan is a question given to you by the Zen master when your practice has reached a certain depth. An example might be, show me your original face before your parents were born. Don't tell me, show me! Koans were the very heart of our practice. As you worked on a koan, you threw away words, concepts and ideas, which easily hypnotize, delude and lead astray. You learned how to break through paradox and confusion, to be with your life and with the nine generations of your family.

At first the koan often seems absurd. Yet it was not absurd; it was vital. And you had to bring an answer. If you did not, or could not, your very life was at stake. Every time you saw the Roshi in dokusan and brought something contrived, you'd be dismissed, time and again. You had to look deeper.

The next time you went to see him, you'd try something else and fail again. Old habits die hard. Failure upon failure piled up fast. These failures were actually good for you; the more the better. It was entirely possible to go on struggling like this with one koan for years. Though it was often humiliating, it was the false ego that was being dismantled. As time passed and failures accumulated, pride diminished and you, yourself, became dissatisfied with a secondhand response. As this went on another part grew, the part that stopped caring about success and failure and was able to live a straightforward life.

A wonderful instruction for working with koans is: "When you are doing zazen sit as though you were a mother hen sitting on her nest, keeping her eggs warm. The mother hen doesn't move or leave the nest alone. When they are ready to be born, the chicks burst through all by themselves."

The koan was no different. One day it burst open. That moment was shocking and life altering. The minute you walked into the dokusan room, the Roshi knew.

I worked on one koan for years. Time after time, I went to

dokusan and brought something cooked up. The moment I said it, the Roshi quickly rang the bell, indicating the interview was done.

Discouragement mounted. I must be crazy, I thought. Or maybe it's him? Maybe he just hates me and doesn't want to say yes to anything? Maybe both of us are crazy? What am I doing here anyway? There's nothing I'll ever be able to do right.

Sesshin was a particularly good time to work on a koan and, discouraged or not, during one sesshin I became determined to solve mine. So, although this particular day I had nothing much to say, and when the bell rang for dokusan, I ran out of the zendo with the others and into the line to wait for my turn.

When the bell rang and my turn came, unexpectedly, I jumped up and flew down the hall.

Then I opened the door to the dokusan room, bowed and blurted out, "I hate my koan, I hate myself."

The Roshi smiled. "Now we're getting somewhere." He seemed unusually pleased. "Now you must redouble your efforts," he insisted. "Work on the koan continually, night and day. Okay?"

"Okay."

For no reason at all I got excited. The koan dug in further. I began to dream about it night after night. It became both a constant companion and also a thorn in my side. At odd moments, it focused me completely, announcing, "Here I am."

19

You're Not Desperate Enough

WHETHER AT SESSHIN OR NOT, I kept working diligently on my koan. Although beautiful moments between myself and the Roshi arrived, most of the time he scowled at me. Whatever I did was never enough, I always slipped up one way or another. The harder I tried, the worse it became and the deeper I fell into the hole of his scorn.

"Not yet, not yet," my great, beloved Samurai Roshi would proclaim, exasperated. "When, Eshin? When?"

Never, I supposed, year after year, as he was still shouting the same thing.

"You're not desperate enough," he hounded us all, "become more desperate. Break through completely. Don't get lost."

I sat on and on, trying to become more desperate, to pass my koans, to gain insight into the deepest truth of life and death. And, of course, to gain the Roshi's respect. After all this time, there was still nothing I longed for more than his respect.

Needless to say, I never could get it—either insight into the deepest truth of life and death or his respect. It never happened. And never would. How could it? Now I realize that only a blind Zen student would sit there waiting and hoping for something like that.

Of course, the Roshi was not interested in giving us respect. What would we do with it? What did we need it for? He was there simply to drive us forward tirelessly to find out the truth for ourselves. Still, students came to him again and again with endless complaints and tales of woe.

"Why do you dwell upon unimportant matters?" he would shout furiously. "Where is life? Where is death? In front of your eyes! Wake up!"

I kept hoping for that precious moment when I would be able to see what was in front of my eyes. What was it, anyway?

"Things are not what they seem, nor are they otherwise." He quoted the great teaching of the Buddha many times. And that much was clear, even to a deluded Zen student like me.

"Sesshin is coming next week," he went on. "If you come, come determined. Don't come to dream or waste your time."

Along with the others, I packed up for that sesshin and went.

"You again?" he said, as I walked through the door.

"Again and again, forever," I mumbled.

He turned his back on me and disappeared.

ॐ ॐ

"BE MORE DESPERATE!" THE ROSHI again demanded in his first talk of the retreat. "How can you ever see through life and death sitting calmly on your cushion dreaming?" His Samurai spirit filled the zendo as it crackled with desperate energy. The bells rang, and the schedule proceeded.

Before long, it was time for dokusan. The bells rang out and the attendant shouted, "Dokusan! Run!"

The zendo emptied out as a fierce flock of students, dressed in robes, elbowed each other out of the way to be first in line to see the Roshi. Each one wanted to be the most the fervent, most desperate, hungry and determined Zen student. The fast runners always got to the front of the line. I usually ended up behind. My legs just didn't run fast enough. Many times I never got to dokusan at all, just sat there waiting, as his bell rang out over and over, and students ran to the dokusan room and then back again. Some looked happy, others forlorn.

But this time, as others were running, I, too, ran like a madwoman. I got to the front of the line and sat there, on the hard wooden floor, in zazen, waiting for that precious moment I would see him alone!

When my turn came, I flew to the dokusan room, entered, knelt before him and stared into his eyes.

"Yessss?" he growled in an odd tone.

I presented my koan and response.

His face curled as if he had bitten on a sour lemon and he shook his head contemptuously, lifted the bell and rang me out of the room.

I had been dismissed literally hundreds of times. But this time I didn't leave. Once again I presented my answer, more strongly.

He laughed.

A moment arose that silenced both of us, totally. We looked at each other and knew. He put the bell down. I sighed.

"Okay," he said, "something, but not yet, not really. It's time to become even more desperate now. March on!"

Trouble Comes

(Everyday Life Sesshin)

20

Dark Clouds Gathering

"Darkness around zendo

New bamboos.

From each leaf rising

Pure wind."

—Soen Roshi

T IMES OF JOY AND SORROW alternate, inevitably. Despite our great joy in practicing together, dark clouds gathered around our zendo. Tales of trouble began to circulate among the students and beyond. Rumors of indiscretion by our teacher arose. People were shocked. Suddenly the zendo was flooded with tears, anger, fear, students leaving, incredible loss. For many it was too hard to stay and sit through this, to reach for a resolution. The Roshi was not the person they'd thought him to be. The very fabric of their practice had been ripped apart.

When I heard the rumors about Roshi's relationship with a woman student, I, too, felt great shock.

"How could it be?" I whispered. The Roshi was married

and his wife was a part of the sangha. We all knew her well. She sat with us, cooked for us and cleaned the kitchen and zendo along with us all. I thought of her silent and stoic manner. She was a powerful force who, in the background, took care of so many things. Many times I would look at her and she wouldn't return my glance. Often she seemed sullen, her jaw firmly set. Now I understood why she felt that way. Did she know about this? What did she feel? She refused to say a word.

As rumors intensified there seemed to be no way to pass through to the other side. I had not seen a sign that anything was happening. The young woman involved had seemed calm and happy all the time. She was close to the Roshi, as were we all.

"How could it be? How could it be?" everyone was asking, and I asked my friend this question as well.

"That's a good question," he shot back. "And there's no decent answer. How dare he do that? I'm getting out of here. This is all a sham."

But it wasn't a sham and I knew it. There was strength here, healing and wisdom. All week long my head spun and I couldn't eat. It was hard to absorb the depth of the koan we had to grapple with now.

As I watched sangha members leave, my heart ripped in two. Where were they going in such disarray? Would they ever find their way back once again? Would they be able to sit so deeply again, the way we all had sat together?

Talk about the relationship between the Roshi and this woman student went on incessantly behind closed doors, on the phones, on street corners and in restaurants. The woman had been a good friend of mine. I wanted to talk to her about it, but she left instantly, without a word to us all. Where had she gone to? I missed her deeply. I called her a few times, but she wouldn't pick up. My questions grew more intense as I spoke to others.

Someone said she left after she found out that she wasn't the only one, felt deceived. Someone else said she'd had a breakdown because of it. Another person said she'd had a breakdown before she ever came and was never as happy and stable as when she was in the relationship with him.

I felt tremendously sad and upset for both her and the Roshi's wife.

"She knew Roshi was married," I stupidly said to a friend there. "What could she have hoped for from this?"

"What kind of idiotic comment is that?" my friend retorted. "Say that to the millions of women who fall in love with married men every day. Some guys lure them in, some don't. Some women enjoy going after married men. Who knows what she was hoping for?"

It made a big difference to me, though. "And what about Roshi's wife," I continued musing. "She saw his wife every day. They worked together in the kitchen."

"It's disgusting, it stinks," my friend replied, "rotten love mixed with incense, who needs it? I'm out of here."

"This has to be very hard for Roshi's wife, too," I said softly then to my friend.

"Maybe it is and maybe it isn't," he responded. "Some say the Roshi told the student he loved her."

"And maybe he did?" I mused.

The person just scowled at me. "That isn't love," he answered.

"What is?" I asked.

"It's not his place to love a student!" My friend grimaced. "He's the teacher here, it's an unequal, power relationship. He can't do that! He's got to be a role model."

Of course I understood what he was saying. No one could argue that. But he was also a human being, sitting with a beating heart.

"But why throw everything away because your teacher has a shocking flaw? This was never a practice of worshipping teachers."

"Say what you want, I couldn't care less." My friend looked at me with disgust. "The practice is ruined for me forever." Then he turned and fled.

Many departed, and as they did I realized that getting out of here wasn't even a possibility for me. The zendo had come to mean far too much. I couldn't bear the thought of life without it. It was hard to know how to proceed.

21

In Love with a Fantasy

THE RUMORS ABOUT ROSHI BROKE out a couple of weeks before a sesshin was to take place. Fortunately I was scheduled to attend and was relieved. It would be a time to sit for hours and work all of it through. A dear friend of mine, James, and I drove up to sesshin, talking constantly about the harrowing events.

"Confront him about it in dokusan," James said heatedly to me.

"How about you?" I asked him.

"You do it," he remarked. "It will be different coming from a woman. Makes more sense."

But what made sense about this? Nothing.

"Are you doing it or not?" James demanded as the car edged closer to the monastery.

"Yes, I'll do it," I replied.

∽ ∾

AS SESSHIN GOT UNDERWAY, THERE was nothing else I could think about. When my turn came to go for dokusan, I decided not to present my koan, but to turn the table and ask him about what he'd done, point-blank.

Finally, the moment arrived. I waited in line until my turn came, then went up into the dokusan room. He sat there as usual on a cushion in zazen. I bowed, entered and sat down on a cushion in front of him.

"Yes?" he asked as usual, expecting me to present my koan and my response to it.

"How could you do this?" I belted out instead.

Shock and horror filled the room.

"Your practice is?" he demanded, trying to get me back on track.

"Tell me why you did this," I demanded.

Suddenly, deep silence fell. "I don't know," he replied then, in a small voice.

We stared at each other.

My head fell into my hands. "Don't know, don't know," I echoed. It was something I deeply understood.

"Don't know," he repeated again and rang the bell. Interview was over. I left.

❧ ❦

THERE IS A WELL-KNOWN ZEN SAYING, *When others are wrong I am wrong.* That saying rang through my mind over and over. After lunch, during the break that afternoon, I went outside and walked on the hillside, alone. As I did I ran into a dear sangha friend, Min. Min was a strong, well-known Korean karate master who had started sitting at the zendo just about when I did. We had become good friends right away, talked a lot, sat together, shared our practice and our lives. Min lived alone and had no personal, romantic relationships. I wondered what he thought about this.

"Min," I cried out the moment I saw him.

He came right over immediately.

"Did you hear?" I could barely talk.

"Yes, I heard," he answered calmly.

"Horrible, awful," I went on.

"This is a great teaching," he went on calmly, "an opportunity to see deeper."

"I have no idea what to do now," I spluttered.

He took a step closer. "Eshin, you worked so hard," he said. "I couldn't have sat with the amount of pain you had in the beginning. But you did, you sat through it. Don't throw all your hard work away now. The lotus flower grows in the mud. You have to put your hands deep into the mud when planting a lotus flower. You can do it. Mud is only mud. Don't let it stop you."

We looked at each other.

"But I loved him so much," I whispered. "How could he do this to me?"

Min looked at me uncompromisingly then. "You didn't love him at all," he responded.

"You loved your fantasy about him. When you can know everything about a person and still love him, then you're doing something. That is love."

A cool breeze from the hills wafted over me as he spoke. I stood enrapt, unable to move. He was right, I realized swiftly. I loved my fantasy about the Roshi, not him. A slow chill ran throughout my body.

At that very moment I knew what my practice would be. To become able to know everything about a person and love them exactly as they were.

ॐ ॐ

USUALLY, WE ARE ASHAMED OF the darkness within, reject ourselves and others because of it, lie about it, exaggerate and build a false front. A great amount of our life force then goes to pretending to be someone we aren't. We pretend to be good and holy, while inside all kinds of feelings stir. Yet, no matter how much we do this, who we really are comes forth. Zen practice lives with and addresses this dilemma at its core.

22

There Are No Enlightened Men or Women

—Joko Beck

THE GAME OF BELIEVING THAT some of us are enlightened and others aren't is a dangerous one. As a wonderful Zen teacher, Joko Beck, once said, *"There are no enlightened men or women, there are only enlightened moments."*

As we practice there are more enlightened moments. There are also many moments of fantasy, delusion, desire, regret. How arrogant to assume that any of us can be exempt from that. And, one might also say, the more deeply embedded our delusions and passions, the more they fuel our need to practice. And the deeper our awareness can become. It's not a matter of good and bad. Zen practice is simply about awakening to all of life as it is.

"Do not depend on others. You are the Light. Depend on Yourself. Don't look outside to an Enlightened man or woman."

It was one thing to read these statements; it was another to make them real in our lives. Of course everyone saw the Roshi as the epitome of an "Enlightened One." No one saw him as an advanced dharma student, practicing along with us. When he behaved badly, naturally, intense disappointment, hatred and anger became focused upon him.

The responses of students were understandable, but the deeper question was how would we respond? Inadvertently, he was making the teachings a living practice for us now. Should we throw him out of our hearts? Had he thrown us out of his heart when we brought all sorts of sadness and bad behavior to him? What was truly needed? How could we find healing for all? This was our natural koan, given to us by life itself. We would not find the answer by escaping, hating, judging, hiding. A deeper response was needed.

As we sit, over time, we stop judging, hating and rejecting the different aspects of ourselves and of others. When we reject and suppress our negativity, it accumulates and sooner or later erupts, creating physical and mental symptoms, painful relationships. What we cannot face or accept in ourselves, we then attack in another. All because we refuse to sit still and taste the bitterness within.

We had placed great expectations upon Roshi. We imagined and demanded that he was stronger, wiser, kinder than anyone else. He was and he wasn't. Along with the great gifts he possessed, he too, struggled and he, too, succumbed. He healed and he hurt. He was healed and destroyed. He was a savior and villain. His behavior gave us our everyday life koan—how do we stop separating what we like from what we dislike and live with it all?

Inevitably, in the midst of deep sitting, soft lights, bells and incense, inhibitions and defenses melt away. The hunger for love, connection and power rises up in all. The craving also arises to be the Roshi's favorite, closer to him than anyone else, to share his strength and wisdom. Longings from childhood become activated. These longings get in the way of many aspects of our lives, and in the zendo we are given the chance to see them and let them go.

But it is also easy to succumb. Although everything arises in deep zazen, it arises to be seen, experienced and to be released, not acted upon. Not always so easy. And this is a great danger of practice. The stronger the practice the more intense the feelings can grow. For the Roshi, too, not so easy.

Many women were drawn to the Roshi's gifts and charisma, and in one way or another offered themselves to him. You could see how the women looked at him, yearned for him, begged to be his in hundreds of ways. Some pursued him intensely, though his wife was right there. Roshi had devoted his whole life to sharing the practice, to teaching. It was easy to see his longing to help others, and also his deep, personal struggle with loneliness within.

"Do not look at the faults of others, look at your own deeds, done and undone," Roshi would tell us, quoting the famous words of the Buddha. "Turn your light within, search your own lives. Blaming others is a deadly trap."

Of course that was true and it was also true that accountability was needed. I am not supporting his behavior, or trying to make it acceptable. None of this is to condone damaging behavior. I do want to look at it more closely though. The same pattern has taken place not only in our zendo, but in many zendos across the country, and also in religious institutions of other kinds.

To do this practice safely, strenuous guidelines and guards are required. When practicing with lay students, a hierarchical monastic model is often unworkable. It is dangerous to vest so much power in one person; it inevitably backfires sooner or later. Students begin to project all their needs upon the teacher. He or she is not a therapist trained to handle what is called transference.

A Zen teacher comes from a completely different point of view. Often the teacher becomes overwhelmed by the emotional demands students make. Confusion is inevitable. This process can become dangerous not only for the students, but for the teacher involved, as well. How to work with this wisely is the great koan all Zen centers and students face today.

Many say that lack of morality is a danger of Zen practice. But the highest moral value in Zen is dissolving delusion, seeing truth and living it. The highest moral action is responding from the deep, inner truth of who you are. Implicit in this is a deep faith that when we discard falseness, lies and hypocrisy, who we are is filled with natural wisdom, compassion and spontaneous healing.

When so-called good and moral behavior is only on the

surface, when one acts one way and feels another, what is left is inauthenticity and confusion. Surface warmth never heals anyone's heart. Surface smiles never banish loneliness. Surface generosity doesn't give anything, but is simply a form of barter. Sometimes what seems to be cruelty brings forth the highest good. Sometimes what looks like compassion is fool's gold, a form of manipulation. How do we know? What can we trust? This is the greatest koan of all.

When we live from this superficial aspect of ourselves a deep lack of reality arises. And the mixed messages we inevitably give forth drive ourselves and those around us crazy. No one truly knows the other, no one truly knows themselves. Then everyone wonders why they feel so disconnected and alone.

Zen practice strips this away—the false games, lies, and with it, certain restraints. This certainly can be dangerous, but it is also dangerous to live a false life, never tasting true love or compassion. Not ever really encountering the one before you or being encountered.

Over and over I tried to bring up the need for more participation by students and accountability in running the zendo. But I wasn't a monk or nun, just a miscellaneous Zen student. I just came and sat and wouldn't leave. In that system, I had no right to say a word. The system of governance here was part of the problem.

And why did I continue on despite this situation which might have seemed utterly hopeless? Because life itself, with its endless changes and fluctuations, seemed hopeless to me without the practice of zazen. There was nothing happening different in the zendo than anywhere else in the world. If I ran from it here, where would that take me? True, I sat at other zendos, met different teachers, learned a great deal from them, but always I returned. The zazen here was different from anywhere else I ever went. My connection with Roshi was deeper. There was no such thing as a flawless teacher. The flaws themselves were the teacher, I finally realized. This was my home, and I felt it, despite the trouble within.

There is no perfect world to do zazen in, I finally decided. Zazen itself creates the perfect world, whatever conditions present themselves. The sitting itself allows us to digest our lives, no matter what is dished out. It allows us to stay strong and clear in the midst of turbulence. If there is a way to change things, we see it and do it. If there is not, we do not muddy the waters, but keep sitting until conditions change.

"Just get out of there," people often said to me when they heard about what was going on. Although I certainly under-stood the desire to escape, I thought of a wonderful story of a Zen master in Japan who ran a large monastery with many monks. All the monks came to notice that one of their brother monks escaped each night over the monastery wall, went into town, stole things and spent the evenings with ladies of ill repute.

Horrified they went to the Zen master and told him about it.

He listened quietly.

The monks insisted that the Zen master chastise this brother monk and throw him out of the monastery, fast.

The Zen master refused.

"If you don't get rid of him, we're going," the righteous monks declared.

The Zen master was unruffled. "It's fine if you want to go," he declared. "You will all do well wherever you go. But your brother monk needs me. Yes, he goes over the wall each night. But then he returns."

> *"The great need before our eyes*
> *Does not allow us to go by the rules."*
> —Book of the Zen Grove

23

Don't Let Go

JUST LIKE LIFE, ZEN PRACTICE is built upon paradox—two sides of a coin, flipping back and forth. Let go and also hold on fast. Hold onto nothing and stay planted. As the cool winds of change come, go with them wherever they lead you. And wherever they lead you, you return to your home.

So what do we let go of, what do we hold onto? I could not let go of my teacher, no matter what I had heard. There was too much I respected about him. He had gifts that were far too rare.

Fierce determination! Every ounce of the Roshi's body and life was based upon fierce determination! He was never late, never missed a sitting, met with students when they needed him, and when they did not, gave wonderful endless dharma talks whether he felt like it or not. He sat like a mountain, holding up the entire zendo even when deep inside he was lonely, sad, tired, forlorn. Even when he felt like a total stranger to this country, others and himself. Even when he wondered what in the world he was doing here—still, he just sat.

Though no one ever knew it, the Roshi was often forlorn. So was I. We both walked to the zendo first thing in the morning, before the light of day dawned, forlorn. He walked a few blocks from his apartment, I walked from mine. For many years and during different eras my apartment was always a few blocks away from his. But, outside of the zendo, I rarely saw him. Almost never. He knew little about my actual life and I knew little about his. I rarely saw him out of his robes or working clothes. He had his job to do, I had mine. And beyond that, he didn't much like me. I was basically an irritant to him.

On the surface it looked like a formal relationship. On the inside I was totally embedded in his heart—and he was embedded in mine. I had no idea how deeply embedded until the trouble escalated, and I could rarely see or sit with him anymore.

When you sit together for years and years something out of your awareness happens. You truly, actually, become one. Or, you live through the oneness you always were. The false sense of separation we live with daily dissolves into the nothingness it truly is.

In Zen practice there is a different notion about what it means to love. When the Roshi got to the zendo, he went up to the third floor and, no matter how he felt, put on his black robe. Just putting the robe on, determination increases. Every morning, every evening, nothing ever kept him away. People came and went but he remained. He sat through every retreat with all his students, from early morning to late at night. There were one-day retreats, weekend retreats, seven-day retreats, year after year after year, season after season. When the bell rang, he was always there. That itself was staggering. That kind of dedication was more than I could fathom. I could feel that dedication to my children, my family, some of my friends. But to the whole world? To strangers and misfits, enemies and stragglers? The zendo doors were opened to them all. He welcomed them, served up zazen and a cup of hot green tea. At the time I didn't realize I, too, had that dedication, locked up inside, waiting to burst through. One of these lifetimes it will happen, maybe, I thought. But now, in this lifetime? Right here, today?

"You come here and complain that no one loves you," Roshi once growled during evening during zazen. "You complain about everything! But what are you talking about? Aren't the doors open every morning and evening? Aren't the floors polished brightly, absolutely clean? Don't flowers await you on the altar? What more are you looking for?"

The wooden floors were always hand polished, immaculate, shining. The room was totally empty of clutter, empty of everything except round, black cushions, lined one next to another on a straw Japanese tatami mat. The cushions were puffed up, clean, waiting for us to sit on them. To sit and sit and sit. Then go home. Someone had grabbed the dust rag to prepare for us all. The ultimate love.

In the zendo love wasn't a word or fleeting emotion. It wasn't a fantasy that curled around your heart and wouldn't let go. Above all, love was not a demand or relentless attachment. It was the fierce determination to practice, no matter what came—no matter what hit you or hurt you, no matter how tired, discouraged or alone you became. Just come to the zendo, put on your robe, sit down on the cushion, face yourself and shut up. That was true love. For yourself and everyone you came in contact with along life's road.

Ultimately that seemed to be the answer to everything. When you put on your robe you were grabbing the dust rag, doing what was needed, sitting strong, accepting whatever came, being a witness, not moving an inch in the midst of it all. Just returning to the still, silent center where everything you needed was waiting for you.

This wasn't psychology, philosophy, anthropology, theology. There were no beliefs to grab onto. This wasn't linguistics, or a place for head games. Although plenty of head games happened, true practice shone a clear light on them all.

"But how can just sitting cure my suffering?" a student begged for understanding. "It doesn't make sense."

"What makes sense?" the Roshi thundered.

"How can it end my suffering?" the student demanded.

"How can it not?" the Roshi replied with unbearable sweetness then. "Just sit and you will see."

What we saw was different from what we expected. On one level, as days and nights went by, often our suffering increased. Cold weather came, storms arose and petered out. People we loved passed away, relationships ended, sickness and pain gripped us. Betrayal by those we held most dear took place. Disappointment grew fiercer and fiercer. And we sat through all of it. Pain may continue, but suffering can come to an end.

It's a great mistake to assume that each one in the zendo doesn't experience every possible human emotion, confusion, delusion—that because we sit we didn't fall down. When we sit deeply we can fall more deeply, more dangerously, perhaps. But one thing we know—how to dig our way up out of every pothole and get back up again. Over and over. Fierce determination.

The Roshi experienced this more deeply than all of us. After all, he was way more committed. He'd given his life over completely to practice, to keeping the zendo going, opening the doors, welcoming everyone in.

Walking into the hollow zendo now, where, due to the difficulty, he is not permitted to enter, I put my palms together and bow. And I remember the words he growled at us, over and over again.

"March on, march on, you are nothing if you do not keep going."

24

The Wheel of Karma

STUDENTS LEFT AND OTHERS ARRIVED. Over and over the seats were filled with new faces. The same drama repeated itself again and again. Call it the wheel of karma, or the repetition compulsion. Whatever you call it, it would have its day.

Although, in the past, I and several others warned new women students that Roshi had a roving eye, and it could cause trouble, no one paid the least attention or seemed to care. And, with all the beautiful women appearing, the same temptations struck again and again. It was like the myth of Sisyphus, a man who strenuously rolled the rock up to the top of the mountain, only to have it roll down again. And then he had to roll it up all over again. And then it rolled down— eternally.

What is this rock Sisyphus struggled with? What is this weight of ignorance, blindness and raw desire that lives inside? Whatever it was, I had great faith in zazen to heal and release it, no matter how long it would take.

As I, too, sat with this rock in my heart, sometimes the rock melted completely and I was free to enjoy the view from the top of the mountain. Other times it rolled right back down and I seemed to be where I started from, the bottom. But as I kept sitting, the top and bottom of the mountain didn't seem so different anymore—first the view from the heights, then the view from the depths. Inevitably there were days of wonderful, compassionate behavior, and then other days of darkness and complaint. No matter what, I kept sitting anyway. This very process is the teaching of zazen.

There is a koan that says, at a monastery snakes and dragons live together, front three three, back three. This points to the fact that snakes and dragons live within us all, completely intertwined, throughout all time. The power, beauty and love are there, and the dangerous aspects as well. Love, deceit and poison are all intertwined. The poison is not to be hated and discarded, though, but to be transformed into the light.

The Bodhisattva's Vow, which we recite every day, describes the essence of our practice, guidelines to dealing with pain and contradiction, which we were called upon to actualize now.

> *"When I a student of Dharma,*
> *Look at the real form of the universe,*
> *All is the never-failing manifestation*
> *Of the mysterious truth of Tathagata.*
> *In any event, in any moment,*
> *And in any place,*
> *None can be other than the marvelous revelation*

Of its glorious light.
This realization made our patriarchs
And virtuous Zen masters extend tender care,
With a worshipping heart,
Even to such beings as beasts and birds.
This realization teaches us
That our daily food and drink,
Clothes and protections of life
Are the warm flesh and blood,
The merciful incarnation of Buddha.
Who can be ungrateful or not respectful
Even to senseless things,
Not to speak of man?
Even though he may be a fool,
Be warm and compassionate toward him.
May we extend this mind over all beings,
So that we and the world together
May attain maturity in Buddha's wisdom."

—Torei Zenji

25

Marching On

"Extraordinary link,
We find each other again
Bright moon."

—Soen Roshi

ARCH ON WAS NOT ONLY a phrase we heard at the zendo again and again, but each year there was a March On sesshin at the monastery during the month of March. It was during the March On sesshin that a Zen master from Japan and his monks arrived yearly to join us for practice.

Usually I did not attend this particular sesshin. But then the time came, and I did. And it was during March On Sesshin that I unexpectedly fell over the cliff. It happened the moment I saw the Zen master that had arrived from Japan.

The moment he walked into the zendo, my body opened and zazen deepened. I went to dokusan with him many times. It was as if I were looking in the mirror with nothing at all in between. The veils were stripped away by themselves.

"You must come to Japan to practice this training period," he said urgently after a few days.

My children were all grown now and had moved away. Our home was sold. I was now back living in an apartment near the zendo, this time alone. Why not go? I thought, and began to make arrangements to go practice with him, do a sesshin at his ancient Zen monastery hidden far up in the mountains. I had heard rumors about the monastery, that it was a rough and difficult place, but did not pay attention to it. This Roshi was so incredibly powerful and yet gentle, all I knew was that I had to go.

My Roshi didn't realize I was going, even though I told him. When I said it to him, the words didn't register, or he just refused to believe me. He never paid attention to anything I said anyway. Once I decided to go, I called him on the phone.

"Roshi, I want to come up to the monastery to talk to you about something," I said.

"Tell me now," he said gruffly over the phone, "I don't have time for you."

"I'm going to Japan for sesshin," I breathed.

He must have thought I was having a fantasy. "Dreams, dreams," he scowled. "We'll talk about it another time."

I packed up and left, having no inkling of what this would mean to him. I thought he'd be proud of my dedication. I thought he'd be pleased by my adventurous spirit. Soen Roshi had passed away a while ago, and I thought of him every day. I felt it would be wonderful and refreshing to study with someone new once again.

I sat at the airport quivering with excitement. Arrangements had been finalized. The Roshi's assistant in Japan was going to come to the airport to pick me up when I arrived. She and I had been emailing and faxing. It was all set.

Going to Japan

26

Don't Get Bitten

T HRILLED, I FINALLY BOARDED THE plane and left for Japan. After years of studying the ancient Japanese masters, I felt as if I were flying home. I was also excited to meet the assistant at the airport when I arrived.

First I had to change planes at Tokyo for another plane closer to the monastery. After traveling for over sixteen hours, I arrived at the airport I was headed to. Exhausted, I got out, gathered my luggage, passed through customs and looked around. The assistant had said she would be there, holding a sign.

No one was there waiting for me. A sea of Japanese faces appeared before me instead. Dazed, I walked into the crowd and did not hear anyone speaking English. I spoke only a few words of Japanese myself. Stranded and exhausted, I looked around desperately.

Finally, another Japanese traveler, seeing my distress, and thankfully, speaking English, came over and assisted me. Together we called the woman who was supposed to be at the airport waiting to pick me up.

She sounded surprised to hear from me. "Oh, I heard your plane would be late," she said. "There's a lot of traffic getting to the airport. I'll be there later. Just wait."

She was coming from a nearby destination and I wondered how much traffic there could be getting to the airport. I thanked the kind traveler for helping, sat down and waited, wondering if she was really going to come.

About an hour later the assistant appeared. Harried, she whisked me away, piled my luggage in her car and told me I was going to spend the night in a small hotel nearby.

"In the morning you'll be picked up and taken to the monastery," she said in a bitter voice.

"Good night."

I had no idea why there was such bitterness toward me. I'd received many faxes from both her and the Roshi there, telling me I was welcome. He had seemed so pleased that I was coming.

First thing in the morning, there was a tough knock on my door. Thankfully, I was ready, not having been able to sleep much the night before.

Three shaven, rough-looking monks nodded at me. One grabbed my luggage and the other nodded for me to follow him. I and my luggage were tossed into the back of a pickup truck, and we started to make our way along the bumpy road up to the monastery.

Through the trees I could see the gorgeous monastery and beautiful grounds. It was as if I were returning to ancient

Japan. The pickup truck entered the gates and as soon as it got far enough, it stopped at the small nun's house along the road threw my luggage inside. Only one other woman lived there, a nun from Germany. She and I looked at each other strangely as I came to join her in her hut.

Who was she? I wondered. Would we ever become friends?

"We must go see the head monk immediately, and tell him you've arrived," she said.

Without settling down or unpacking, I quickly followed her through the exquisitely cared for grounds, along pebbled paths to the head monk's office.

The head monk didn't look up when we walked in. Just grunted in Japanese.

"I've arrived," I said boldly.

He looked up at me disdainfully. "For how long?" he replied in English, displeased.

"About a month, I guess," I replied.

"Huh," he said unintelligibly. Then he motioned to the nun beside me. "Give her work assignment. Start immediately." Nothing further to be said, he looked down again.

We walked back down to the nun's quarters silently. When we got there, she told me to immediately start pulling out the weeds all around the hut. There had been a lot of rain and the weeds had grown wildly. There was not a moment to waste.

"Get going," she demanded.

Just pull weeds, just grab the dust rag, I thought as I got down on my hands and knees and start looking for the slender weeds to pull out. The blazing sun was hot and I was exhausted. The nun didn't say another word to me, just went inside smugly.

No support, no warmth, nothing to depend upon. This was a radical practice of a basic Zen teaching: Do not lean on others! Cut the leaning, depending mind. Depend on yourself! You are the Light, do not waver, do not doubt.

I had no idea how long I should keep pulling the weeds. There seemed to be no end to them or to the heat that grew stronger and stronger, pounding down on me.

Finally, she came outside. "You missed this patch here," she exclaimed in a harsh tone.

"Finish that up and come back inside."

I finished up and went back inside, sweaty and dirty.

"There's not much water, so use it carefully when you wash," she instructed. "And when you walk on the grounds, be mindful. There are dangerous insects here creeping around, Mukade, poisonous centipedes. If you are bitten you will die in an hour, so let us know immediately."

My entire body turned into ice. "Who should I let know? Nobody's around."

At that she finally smiled lightly. "Exactly," she replied. "Everyone's busy, they're hard to find. So, stay wide awake. Don't get bitten and bother us all."

The practice of life and death was not a game here, not a saying or a joke. You took your life in your hands. If you did not practice strongly, anything could happen. And if you did practice strongly, anything could happen as well.

I looked pleadingly for sympathy from the nun then, but she immediately turned her back. It's happening all over again, I murmured to myself. I can't stand her and she can't stand me.

27

Nothing to Depend On

ACH MOMENT, EACH STEP AT the monastery, was choreographed like an ancient dance. You had to quickly learn exactly how to take off your shoes, where to leave them, how to bow, how to eat, which hand went first in scooping up the wet, sticky, tasteless rice. Food here was not a pleasure or comfort to look forward to or depend upon. You had to know how many pickles to take with each meal. If you messed up you were yelled at and hit.

Naturally clumsy, I couldn't do any of it. I couldn't figure out which hand went first or second, and exactly, precisely how to bow. When I made a mistake (as I did constantly) I was shoved and pushed into the right positions. Frustrated, many times the nun dug her nails into my shoulders and grabbed me again and again.

At one point, seeing the horror on my face, she said, "Sorry, but I have to behave this way, or I will not be respected by the monks."

This was her territory I had charged into, not knowing where I was going or how to behave. And I still hadn't seen the

Roshi there who had insisted that I come. We still had to have our formal greeting meeting. Would he help me through this maze? I wondered. But soon I began to doubt. This was training going on, ancient Zen training. Very different from reading about it in a book.

When the Roshi and I finally had our greeting meeting, I felt as though I'd fallen into a field of lilies. Just being with him was thrilling and comforting. He spoke softly and we both smiled. I felt the dharma teachings and ancestors surrounding us all around.

Silent and majestic, he smiled at me. "Welcome," he said softly.

I savored the moment and always will. "Thank you, thank you," I answered.

Somehow, this Roshi and I understood one another. When he was nearby I could sit longer and longer without pain. Koans did not seem impermeable. Life took on a different hue. Just who he was seemed to be the answer I'd been seeking all my life.

Although he spoke fine but limited English, I understood all the words he said and also the ones he never uttered.

"And how are you doing?" he asked quietly, then.

It was the wrong question at the wrong time. Foolishly, I tried to tell him about what was happening and how hard it was for me.

For a moment he looked surprised, then offended. "Why are you telling me this? Tell the head monk," he instructed.

JUST GRAB THE DUST RAG

There were layers and layers of hierarchy, structure and formality here. Paths went in one direction only, and never wavered.

Tears filled my eyes. He looked away. This was not something he was used to.

FINALLY, AFTER DAYS OF TRYING to keep the schedule, sleeping little, making constant mistakes, being pushed, shoved and yelled at, I couldn't eat, couldn't sleep. And the sesshin hadn't even begun. My body rhythms were unraveling. And as time went on, things only intensified and got worse. I truly did not see how I could sit through a seven-day sesshin in this state. I just couldn't do it. The escape artist rose up within me, telling me it was time to go.

"Time to leave," I announced to the nun, late that afternoon during the short rest period.

She looked at me in horror. "Leave? You just arrived a few days ago."

"And now I'm leaving," I replied quickly.

"No, you're not. What do you think this is? Some kind of game?"

"I am sick," I said. "I can't eat, I can't sleep. I'll never be able to make it through sesshin in this state and I don't want to disturb anyone."

"You've already disturbed everyone." She gritted her teeth. "Why did you come in the first place?"

I was struck with horror by her question, felt as though I had infringed upon everything here, failed completely. I just turned away and with tears in my eyes, started packing.

"Please ask the monks to call me a taxi," I asked her.

"Giving up just like that?" she asked. "Demoralizing everyone?"

Say what you want, I thought, I'm getting out of here.

It wasn't so simple though. They refused to call a taxi for me. It had to be approved by the Roshi. He was also stunned and had no idea why I wanted to depart so quickly. Not knowing what else to do, he finally sent down a tiny container of vanilla ice cream for me.

Starved and parched, I ate it hurriedly. That little container of vanilla ice cream was the most delicious ice cream I'd ever had, but I still wanted to go home. I turned back to packing.

"If you go, you may never, ever, ever return." The nun glared at me, shocked and disturbed by the ice cream as well.

Just get me out of here, I thought to myself. Why in the world would I want to return?

☙ ❧

FINALLY, ABOUT SIX HOURS LATER, after discussion back and forth, they called a taxi. Grateful, I took my luggage, climbed in and looked out of the car window as we drove back to the small hotel I'd started in.

I was never so happy to see any place in the world. One more stop and I'll be flying home, I foolishly imagined. The hotel was extremely simple, but yet had a wonderful restaurant on the second floor. And each room off the narrow corridors had a real bed and bath of its own. All this time I'd been sleeping on the floor and the prospect of lying down in a real bed seemed like a gift from heaven. I was shocked to realize how I'd taken something as simple as that completely for granted before.

I checked in quickly and, thrilled to be in a room of my own, immediately drew a hot bath. After soaking in it thoroughly, I climbed out and practically swooned onto the slim, wobbly bed. In a moment I was in a deep sleep, deeper than I could ever remember.

When I awoke in what seemed like hours later, I changed my clothes and went down to the restaurant to order dinner. I would make arrangements for return tickets back home in the morning, I decided. Then, after checking the menu, I savored a bowl of completely unexpected, delicious spaghetti, which I never expected to find here in Japan.

࿅ ࿆

FIRST THING IN THE MORNING, after breakfast, I went back to my room and started making calls to book a flight home. Suddenly, there was a knock on my door. I jumped up, opened it quickly and to my shock, there stood the Roshi's assistant, the woman who had picked me up at the airport. Now she was smiling and as sweet as could be.

"I heard you are planning a trip home," she said nicely, in

the doorway.

"Yes," I replied quickly.

"Please come with me for a bite in the restaurant," she went on. "I'd like to talk to you about it."

Of course there was no way I could refuse. Just a few days ago she had picked me up at the airport and here I was now going home. I could see how troubling this could be.

During the meal, she told me that if I left this way, it would look terrible for my Roshi back home. I would be shaming him, shaming everyone, creating terrible karma for all. It would be far better to stay here until sesshin ended. Sesshin was to start in two days. I could sleep at the junior college down the hill and take my meals there. Then I could walk up the hill to the monastery and join in the sesshin. After sesshin was over, I could leave honorably. Her intense eyes shone into mine.

Return to the monastery? I shuddered. But I did not want to create difficulty, either here or back home. And I'd come all the way to Japan to do the sesshin. I still wanted to do that, just didn't know how I'd be able to. I was amazed that they were willing to make so many adjustments for me to make it possible. I looked into her eyes and into my heart and had no choice but to agree.

"Yes, of course I'll return," I said simply.

"Wise decision," she said as her voice suddenly rose an octave.

Before I knew it, I was packed up again and crammed next to her in a small car, heading along the bumpy roads, back up to the monastery. I had no idea, though, that from her point of view, she was transporting a passenger of shame. She just wanted to get me there, take me to my new room at the junior college down the hill, give me some orientation and get away as fast as she could.

28

Thrown into My Coffin

I WAS SHOCKED AND PROUD that I had returned. But the moment I went down the hill to the monastery, I could see that others didn't feel the same way.

The head monk greeted me, snarling. "Come with me," he said in rough English, barely looking at me at all.

I followed him down a hill, over to a separate entrance of this ancient monastery, where great masters of the past had come to practice, struggle with blood and tears to gain the jewel of no price. From the look on his face I knew I had no right to be here.

Then, suddenly, without warning, he grabbed me by my shoulders and threw me into a small, dark room. There was one cushion on the floor for zazen, no windows or light. I felt as though I'd been tossed into a dungeon.

"Sit," he hollered, "do zazen by yourself!" His voice so loud it broke through every crevice of my mind.

"Alone?" I was terrified.

"Just sit. When the time comes, I'll open the door." His voice grew darker.

"Wait a minute," I gasped.

"There are no more minutes left, nothing to ask for!" he yelled, as he turned, stormed out and slammed the door behind him so hard I felt as though I'd been thrown into my coffin forever. I had no idea if I would ever come out again.

As if I were dying, my life rolled out before me. What had it amounted to? Where was I now? It was totally dark inside and I had no idea if he'd ever return to open the door. I sat with no sense of time passing and no one to say a word to. I sat without a sense of where I was, or if I'd ever again see the ones I loved. Was I alive? Was I dead? The words that my Roshi had said so many times became vividly real. "Without knowing who you really are, you are nothing but a ghost haunting valleys and hills." Was that what had become of me now? Was I only a ghost here, haunting the hills?

Waves of terror alternated with great sadness. How had this happened? Snatched out of life suddenly, tossed into my coffin with nothing to do but face myself. There was truly nothing left to depend upon except zazen and prayer. In that moment, the two of them became one. I sat, I prayed, I begged for forgiveness. For what? For everything and for everyone.

In the midst of the endless darkness, suddenly I heard the sound of a great gong ringing outside over the hills. Along with the gong, I heard monks chanting the Lotus Sutra. I knew that every day at five they rang the gong and chanted. I clung to the sound of the chanting desperately, let it totally encompass me, listening to it for my very life. Soon zazen went deeper and deeper. Time disappeared then, along with hope, confusion and fear.

In what seemed like only a few minutes the door to the room suddenly flung open, and the head monk, a lit flashlight in his hand, tossed a young woman into the room with me.

"Here, she is a student from the college," he uttered. "She will sit with you, keep you company." Then he left again, slamming the door shut.

In the darkness I looked over at the young, slender Japanese woman who went to her cushion willingly and sat perfectly still, opposite me. Had she volunteered for this odd assignment? I had no idea.

I got up then and did kinhin slowly in the tiny room. She got up when I did and followed along behind. After a short period of walking, we both went back to our cushions to resume zazen.

When the door opened again, the monk growled that this young woman could walk me back down to the college for the night to sleep. He would give her a flashlight to watch for Mukade along the dark road. The next day when we returned, we did not have to sit here, we could continue to do zazen in an attendant's closet (the Jisha) down the hall. I was to sit in the closet for the remainder of sesshin. The young woman would stay with me for another day and then go. There was no room for me in the zendo. Someone like me definitely could not sit there with the monks. I did not deserve it. Oddly, whatever he said didn't matter to me at all.

The next day, the Jisha's closet seemed like a luxury hotel. It had screened doors that looked out onto a rock garden, with plenty of light coming in. What more could one ask for? The cleaning equipment was in the back of the closet, but the young woman and I were given two cushions, near the screened doors where the light came in.

"She will only be sitting here with you for another day," the head monk reminded me. "After that she goes to Kyoto, and you are on your own. When the bells ring out for dokusan, you may leave this room and go in line outside to see the Roshi." He looked at me fiercely. His stern face did not bother me in the least though now. In fact, I smiled.

"Thank you, thank you," I said and meant it.

"For what?" He looked furious and amazed.

29

Apples Given, Oranges Received

I SAT ALL THROUGH THE seven-day sesshin in the Jisha's closet, deeply connected and deeply alone. The lovely young woman left, but it was as if she were still there. Her strong spirit remained behind. No coming, no going. Several times a day, when the bells rang for dokusan, I ran outside for a meeting with the Roshi. The dokusan line was right near the Jisha's closet, so I got there right away. As I took my seat at the front of the line, I heard the monks' feet rushing along the wooden floors from the zendo, to be next in line.

This Roshi never once mentioned that I'd left and returned. Nothing else mattered, only practice, practice, practice. In dokusan with him, all the koans melted into one. Ancient encounters in the silence.

ॐ ৯

ONE NIGHT, AFTER ZAZEN, AS I was sitting on the floor outside the Jisha's closet pulling on my shoes, ready to head back up to the junior college to sleep, the head monk edged over to me. He looked at me out of the corner of his eye.

"Good," he grumbled under his breath.

I looked up at him, amazed.

"Good job," he repeated as our flickering eyes suddenly met.

No other words of praise ever touched me so deeply.

I put my palms together in thanks. He simply grumbled something else, and scuttled along.

ॐ ॐ

FINALLY, THE SEVEN DAYS WERE done, passing like a soft breath wafting by. Time then for the parting meeting with the Roshi. We sat in the room together and bowed. He had hoped I'd stay longer. I could not. He mentioned that perhaps I might return each year at cherry blossom time. At that moment I thought it was possible and agreed happily.

Now I wonder how many lifetimes of cherry blossoms blossoming will have to pass before I can return again.

> *"Friends' faces,*
> *Reluctant to part,*
> *Spring wind."*
>
> —Soen Roshi

ॐ ॐ

FINALLY, IT CAME TIME FOR my taxi to come and take me to the airport back home. The rainy season had started and it was pouring outside. I was sitting in the back of the car, my luggage piled beside me. The rain slashed at the windows as I sat, waiting to get going, when suddenly from the corner of my eye, I saw what seemed to be dark shadows pass alongside the car.

Quickly, I turned, looked out the foggy windows and saw some of the monks I had seen at the monastery, lined up, walking barefoot in straw sandals, in their robes, one behind the other, down to the village, doing takahatsu (begging for alms) in the pouring rain. They wore nothing but thin robes and straw hats, and carried empty begging bowls in their hands. Their bare feet, scratched by weeds, walked through pebbles and dirt, unprotected and unclothed. I sat there dry in the car, beside my bulging suitcases, suddenly filled with horror at myself and my life. There I was sitting warm and dry, carrying all this unnecessary baggage along.

A beautiful, ancient part of Zen practice is takahatsu. This is the time when monks put on straw sandals, wear straw hats with large brims, form a line and go on foot, one behind the other, down into the villages with their begging bowls. The villagers can hear the monks coming from a distance as they chant "Ho, ho, ho" over and over again.

When the villagers hear the chanting, they know the monks are coming to receive offerings. The monks never ask directly. They simply stand with their begging bowls chanting. When a villager comes to make an offering, the monk and villager bow to one another at the same time. Due to the large straw hat the monk is wearing, he cannot see who is making the offering, nor can the person see the face of the monk. The giving and receiving are done anonymously. The giver does not become inflated, thinking how wonderful it is that he gives. The one who receives is not shamed, feeling he is needy. The monk is giving the villager the gift of having an opportunity to share. The villager is providing sustenance for the monk who chants, meditates and cares for him. There is no separation; in this moment, the giver and receiver become one. Indeed, if we go a little deeper, we can even ask, what is it that really belongs to us? What is the true gift being given?

As I watched the monks wind their way down the hill, I knew that I'd received a gift that went beyond anything I was deserving of. And I knew the deeper question was, how would I ever repay it? What could I give back in return?

"Touching one another

Each becomes

A pebble of the world."

—Soen Roshi

Returning Home

(Karma Unfolding)

30

Kicked Out of the Zendo

WHEN I RETURNED FROM JAPAN and the Roshi discovered that I'd actually gone to Japan without his permission, his horror and anger knew no bounds. I was kicked out of the zendo. Forget about marching on then, I could barely stand up and walk.

"Eshin is weak-minded, foolish, has made great trouble," he announced to the students in a public talk. "She has created a disturbance in Japan and had no authorization to go there. You don't take a trip like that lightly."

Someone mentioned to him that I'd been invited by the Roshi there. He just brushed it off. I needed his approval and he hadn't given it to me. I had no right to attend the sesshin in Japan. I was a lay student, not ordained, not sufficiently trained or committed. Beyond that, I'd caused him shame. East and West, West and East, I had no idea that this would have caused him shame. I thought he'd be pleased and proud of me.

Friends gave me reports of the many things he said about me.

I packed up and moved out of the city, to be away from

both him and the zendo. But, go where you like, ties so deep do not easily become undone.

"There are plenty of other teachers you can study with," friends tried to console me. "Zen has become popular now, the teachers are all over the place."

"You don't shop for a teacher the way you shop for a new coat," I murmured, thinking of the deep power that had drawn me to Japan. "A teacher appears. He or she is destined. The connection is beyond what can be imagined. It doesn't go away, either, no matter how he or she behaves."

My friends shook their heads. "All of this is too much. We don't understand any of it, but we're very sorry for you."

Socially speaking, it was all too much. Karmically speaking, inevitable.

೦೩ ⊰

I SAT AND LIVED ALONE for many months, absorbing it all. Some sangha friends came to join me and sit with me in my new home. Reports came to me about the anger I had stirred up at the zendo and the talks about me that went on and on. Some were lies, some were opinion. I sat through them just the way I'd sat in my coffin in Japan.

One year later, the door to my dungeon opened, and it was time, once again, to march on. I got up one morning and out of the blue decided to return to the zendo to sit. Where else could I go? What was life without the practice? Just phenomena dancing without a center. Just love without a heart to land in.

The Roshi scowled terrifically when he saw me. "You again? I see our karma has not yet combusted."

"No, I guess it hasn't," I replied.

31

Some of You We Can't Get Rid Of

NOBODY COULD BELIEVE I'D ACTUALLY returned to the zendo, even me. But I did and fairly soon I felt as though nothing had ever happened. I was where I belonged, sitting on the cushion, chanting, walking, having tea with dharma friends. The only difference was, the Roshi's scowls didn't bother me at all, nor did the way he purposely tried to ignore me. Mosquitoes on a summer night, I thought, biting away under the moon. Let him scowl all he likes. Who cares if he sits like a mountain, is wrapped in black silk robes and walks along the floor, his feet brushing the wood like a golden hawk? He's simply another dharma student, sitting on the cushion with us all.

One day during weekend sesshin, he gave a talk, looking at me the whole time.

"Some of you come to the zendo for one night, others for one month, others a year. Some come for about three years or so. Then there are some we cannot get rid of."

That was me and I knew it. I was proud. Was he saying I was a determined Zen student? Was this his way of complimenting me? I wondered about it every day until early one evening, when I arrived for zazen. I was taking my shoes off and putting them carefully in the wooden shoe rack when an American monk who lived there came over and looked at me sadly.

"You know, Eshin, there are other zendos," the monk said, haltingly.

"Sure," I replied offhandedly, not really knowing what he was getting at.

Good thing I didn't understand. It takes a kind of stupidity to keep going, a stupidity that keeps you on the cushion, no matter what. This stupidity that allows you to go deeper and deeper, overlook discouragement, bitterness and the natural failings of us all.

And, then, hopefully one day, that stupidity turns into a joy that surpasses smart and stupid, right and wrong. It shines by itself, on everything!

"Did you ever think…" the monk started to stammer.

I spun around and we looked at each other plainly. "What?"

"Some say you're stalking the Roshi!" the monk burst out.

"He can't stand me?" I asked simply.

"Well…" The monk hesitated.

"Too bad," I replied. "He'll get over it. I have deep faith in our zazen."

꙰ ꙰

THEN THE GREAT EARTHQUAKE AT our zendo happened. By then,

most of us who practiced in New York thought that our Roshi's problems with the women had ended. It never came up, was a non-issue. Then suddenly, like an unexpected storm, the problem burst forth once again. Burst forth with such vehemence that the Roshi, too, had to depart.

In the horror and shock for all of us, in the blame and rage that came pouring down upon our zendo, there was great difficulty holding onto our practice. At times it was almost impossible to remember what we had found there. The very fabric of our practice was being questioned. What's the good of sitting so much if this is what comes of it? many asked. Is the practice being used for denial, or selfish gains? Is there a lack of concern and compassion here for the women who had been shocked, disappointed and harmed? What's the good of it then?

Huge questions that will and must reverberate deeply, and be responded to. These questions must cause us to look carefully at the nature of our sitting, depth of compassion and what truly constitutes compassion and harm. Gain and loss, healing and harm—can they be separated? Were these women victims of a dark force? Did they play a part in this dangerous dance? Is blame useful, or deep acceptance of responsibility by all, along with a longing to create true healing and structures that support well-being?

This kind of inquiry has yet to unfold. The rage and blame directed not only toward the Roshi, but all of us, went on unabated, taking inspiration away. But without our inspiration to sit, we're finished. Above all we have to guard our inspiration carefully, remember the principals our practice was founded upon: acceptance, forgiveness, recovery from error. And most importantly, marching on!

This is not to say that changes do not have to be made; they do. But how can they without an atmosphere of clarity and compassion for all?

"I am never upset for the reason I think."
　　　　　　　　　　　　—A Course in Miracles

32

Times of Change

"The whole world is medicine,
What is the illness?"

A S ZEN PRACTICE IS BEING planted in the West, a time of change has come. Now many little sanghas have cropped up, with friends sitting together at each other's homes. Although the practice requires guidance, those who guide our practice come in all forms. The danger of making a teacher into an infallible being has become more and more clear. New models are needed.

In the San Francisco Zen Center one of the protections is to change the abbot each year. Hierarchical systems where the leader is accountable to no one but a board of their choosing is coming to an end. This autocratic model is dangerous for all concerned.

The Zen Mountain Monastery has managed to travel this road beautifully. The monastics there have made a lifelong commitment, and though they have a strong monastic system, the great integrity of their practice and true concern for sangha keeps it thriving and alive.

The need for teachers who give interview to have some psychological understanding is also becoming clearer. As mindfulness practice becomes more mainstream, it is important to realize the power and depth of what can emerge and how to handle it wisely. A teacher needs to be familiar with the process of transference, whereby a student projects onto those in authority childhood images, wishes and longings. And where a teacher can also easily get caught in projecting his or her wishes as well. This is a natural, perhaps inevitable process and must be handled with skillful means.

It is also important to realize that zazen practice is far more than a tool for feeling better—though feeling better is often a wonderful side effect. Zazen practice does not exist to remove symptoms, but to go to the root of suffering and pull it out. When we deal simply with branches, we cure one symptom and then another arises. When the root is pulled out, true healing appears.

How to go forward is a great koan many of us are facing these days, how to find a true teacher?

Who Is the True Man of No Rank?

This question is a well-known koan. It points to the fruits of practice, and describes the Zen man or woman living a fulfilled life, dedicated to the well-being of all. This person will not necessarily be found in temples, churches, or wrapped in robes. She may be indistinguishable from others, standing behind you in line in the supermarket or in the booth behind you in the coffee shop. How will you find her? How will you know? This person will not ask you to bow down to him or her, to become attached or idolize them, but they will return you to your own freedom and joy.

Nyogen Senzaki, one of the founders of Zen in America, was a lay person. He worked all day and held Zen meetings in his apartment at night. He called his zendo The Mentogarten, meaning the kindergarten. Students had to go back to the beginning, to kindergarten, and start all over again. Everyone has learned so much over the years, but many miss discovering the important things. If you wanted to regain the wisdom you had as a child, you went and sat with him.

Kyudo Roshi, a successor of Soen Roshi, had a zendo in Manhattan for a while. Plain and direct, his practice was completely rooted in everyday life. He helped cook for sesshin, did his own shopping, cleaned the zendo impeccably and always focused upon the student's life. And in the midst of everyday life, no matter what happened, nothing ever deterred Kyudo Roshi from the practice of zazen.

My friend Constantin was a student of Kyudo Roshi for many years. In all that time, however, he'd never asked him a question. Finally, Constantin made an appointment to speak with Kyudo Roshi for one September evening, at five p.m.

That day, to the entire world's horror, turned out to be September eleventh, and Kyudo Roshi's zendo was not far from the World Trade Center. Through the chaos that ensued,

Constantin called Kyudo Roshi to tell him that of course, he could not come.

When Kyudo Roshi picked up the phone, he did not give Constantin time to say anything. "I'll see you at five o'clock," he declared.

"But Roshi," Constantin spluttered, "how will I get there? There are blockades everywhere."

"Just get here," Kyudo Roshi replied and hung up the phone.

He probably doesn't realize what's going on, thought Constantin, and quickly called him back again. "Roshi, there's been terrible trouble."

"Trouble or no trouble—just be here at five," Kyudo barked and hung up again.

Amidst the terror that gripped the city, incredulous, Constantin began winding his way on foot downtown. Finally, somehow, he made his way through the blockades to the street the zendo was on. Then he walked over, rang the bell and was buzzed in.

Shocked to see the Roshi under these conditions, Constantin climbed the stairs and walked in.

The Roshi offered him a cup of tea, and the interview proceeded. Time passed and before Constantin realized, it was almost six o'clock, the time when the zendo normally opened for evening zazen.

"Okay, time to get ready for zazen now," the Roshi declared, looking at the clock.

"But Roshi," Constantin interrupted, "no one will be coming tonight."

The Roshi looked at him, unruffled. "It doesn't matter if someone comes or not," he answered promptly. "It doesn't matter what happens out there, when the time comes for zazen, we sit."

In the monastery, or out of the monastery, fierce determination.

Before Kyudo Roshi left to return to Japan and become the next abbott of Ryutakaji Monastery, we were concerned about the future of practice here and turned to him for guidance.

"So many problems, so much confusion," we said. "How do we proceed? What do we do?"

"Help one another," he said. "Keep helping one another and you'll find out."

"Coolness in mountain temple

Dharma net now spread

East and West."

—Soen Roshi

Everyday Life Zen Masters

Cherry Blossoms

"All beings are flowers,
Blooming,
In a flowering universe"

—Soen Roshi

33

Meeting the Master

"Don't put a head on your own head,
What's wrong with your head anyway?"
—Senzaki

C ALL YOURSELF WHAT YOU LIKE, I know you. I see you, dressed in all kinds of clothes, doing all kinds of jobs, appearing everywhere. Inside or out of the zendo, your eyes sparkle, your voice is sound and clear. My teachers are all around me, forever.

If I look closely, if I really listen, cherry blossoms are falling everywhere.

❧ ❧

THE GREAT ART OF MANIFESTING practice in life, and manifesting life as practice, cannot be overstated. Apart from life there is no practice. Sitting in the zendo is of great importance, but then we must step out of the carefully constructed patterns and confront the wild, sprawling, untamable world—and all who are brought to us in it. How do we encounter life? What does it ask of us? How do we respond? Do we still hate and blame those we think have wronged us? If so, we have not yet even started to truly sit. We have not yet even seen a glimmer of how to bring the great blossom of training to shine everywhere.

So many of us make a separation between our spiritual practices, our families and our work in the world. However, if we look closely enough, there is totally no difference between them. Everything that happens is our teacher, everyone we encounter has wisdom to share. It is only us, our eyes are closed, we cling to roles, and are blinded by them. Our children, families, colleagues, patients and friends are truly our teachers. If we let go of our preconceptions long enough and allow them to be who they are, there is no end to the surprises we'll receive and the teachings they will give us.

In the deepest sense, each one we meet is our master and teacher. Each one we meet shows us how to grow. Training continues endlessly. Be careful of those who suggest they've completed training or that they know more than you. Just please grab the dust rag and lovingly care for your world. Do it thoroughly, completely and without complaining. Then perhaps one day, one moment, you may become a true beginning Zen student, after all.

34

Last Day of Rohatsu Sesshin (Don't Force Me to Sit)

"Do Not Squander Your Life"

E VERY YEAR I WENT UP to the monastery for the last sesshin of the year, Rohatsu Sesshin.

This sesshin was conducted in December to commemorate the Buddha's enlightenment on December eighth. Monasteries and Zen groups all over the world gathered to sit together for seven days and nights in honor not only of the Buddha's enlightenment, but, hopefully, of their own.

Rohatsu sesshin was particular rigorous, with longer sittings, colder weather and intense admonitions not to waste a precious moment.

"Sit strong! Don't move a muscle!" the head monk called out again and again in the deepening silence.

Many participants sat through the night, and in some places in Japan, during Rohatsu sesshin the monks were not permitted to lie down to sleep for a full seven days. They slept sitting on their cushions for about three hours during the night. Wherever and whenever Rohatsu sesshin was held, the atmosphere was dedicated and intense.

I particularly loved this sesshin and especially having my birthday fall upon the last day. What a wonderful way to end one year and greet the next. Year after year at Rohatsu sesshin, Roshi gave me a box of incense, both as a gift for my birthday and to continue on for the next year.

One year, to my regret, just having had eye surgery, I could not drive up to the monastery, or sit for the entire week. By the end of the week, I would be better though, and could sit at least for the last day. Although no one came and went during sesshin, due to my situation, they agreed to allow me to come at the end.

So when one of my sons, Adam, asked what I wanted for a birthday gift that year, I said there was nothing more I'd love than for him to drive me up for sesshin for the last day.

He looked slightly downcast. "That's what you want? That's it?"

"Yes," I said, "more than anything."

Reluctantly, he agreed.

All the way up, Adam reminded me that he was only the driver, and had no intentions of joining in to sit. Please don't ask him to. Please don't pressure him. Of course I understood. Although, over the years, Adam had sat a bit at my home-grown zendo, I realized he could not possibly do such rigorous sitting—especially on the last day of Rohatsu, when the intensity was at its peak. As we drove along I reassured him he could find a place to rest at the monastery until the time came to drive home.

As arranged, Adam and I arrived during the lunch break. The moment we walked to the entrance, we were immediately greeted by Pawel, a senior Zen student.

"Okay, okay, hurry up and come in," Pawel said in a throaty tone. "It's almost time for the next sitting."

Adam looked at me out of the corner of his eyes, somewhat alarmed. The intensity and urgency in the air was palpable.

We were quickly shown to our rooms, where we left our bags, and then Pawel took us straight to the zendo to show us where our seats would be.

To my horror, two seats had been prepared, one for Adam and one for me. Both were at the end of the row. Meal bowls and tea cups were also carefully placed right behind our seats, along with plaques with our names on them. A long Shoji screen separated my seat and Adam's, so he would be sitting right behind me. The exquisite care that had been taken to welcome us was overwhelming.

Adam looked at his seat, at the zendo and the preparation that had gone on.

"You'll be sitting here," Pawel said to him, pointing to his seat again.

"Thank you," Adam replied softly. "I appreciate it."

I looked at Adam out of the corner of my eye, hoping he didn't think I'd arranged this. I hadn't.

But Adam was not looking at me. He was gazing at his seat and at the plaque with his name on it, tremendously moved that it was there, waiting for him.

Wooden clappers started sounding, announcing that the

afternoon sitting was to begin.

"Okay, time for zazen," Pawel informed us briskly. "Sit down."

To my complete amazement, Adam simply took his seat. How is he going to do this on the last day of sesshin? I wondered, in fear. What will happen now?

I took my seat as well and felt Adam close behind me, on his cushion. All during the sitting I wondered how he would ever get along. Would he run out suddenly filled with pain, hold this against me forever? To my complete amazement, when I saw him during kinhin, walking along with everyone, it was as though he'd been here his whole life. A little smile on his face, he joined in every sitting and activity for the rest of sesshin.

I watched Ada, as, plucked out of one world and into another, he ate his meals, washed his bowls and sat strongly, focused and at ease. One moment insisting he would not sit, the next, here he was, completely at home. All day long I marveled. I hadn't even known it, but right under my nose, I'd been living with an everyday life Zen master, hidden from sight.

> *"Along this road*
> *Goes no one;*
> *This autumn evening."*
>
> —Basho

35

One Day You'll Never See Me Again

ALTHOUGH HE DIDN'T KNOW IT, and neither did I, now I realize that my father was a great Zen teacher for me. All the struggles we had drove me straight to the zendo, where I encountered the same struggles all over again. But beyond the struggles, and what seemed to be difficulty, my father refused to define himself through the eyes of others. He insisted upon living from his own sense of himself. And he was nobody's fool either; he gave top advice to his law clients, treated each one of them beautifully and always saw a situation through to the end.

Very soon after he opened his own law office, more and more people started to come. All kinds of people, he didn't separate one from another, all were welcome.

Some people in the neighborhood looked at him strangely. "What kind of clientele are you taking in there?"

"Everyone deserves a chance," my father insisted, "and I'm giving it to them."

My father didn't go downstairs to sit outside on the front bench with others either, but spent a lot of time alone, upstairs on the front porch. Night after night he sat quietly under the branches of the old cherry tree, gazing at the sky. Sometimes, I went out there to keep him company.

"I won't be here forever," he told me over and over. "One day you'll all wake up and I'll be gone. You'll never see me again."

Naturally, my first reaction was terror. "Don't go," I begged him.

"I have to," he said. "Other places are calling me. There are places to go, fabulous places with people who look you right in the eye."

My heart clenched. Where were these places? Who would he meet there? Was he saying one day he would suddenly leave me, that my world wouldn't always stay the same?

"In fact, "my father continued, determined, "I'm packing a bag and putting my new suit in it, the one with the blue lapels. Yup, I'm going tomorrow, and I'm packing tonight."

But when tomorrow came nothing was packed.

"So when are you going?" I would continually ask.

He only grinned.

"And when are you returning?" I continued.

"What difference does it make?" he replied. "You can't leave me and I can't leave you, even if we want to. Whether I'm here or not, we are with each other forever. Coming and going don't mean a thing."

36

Take Me As I Am

HOW WOULD I HAVE SURVIVED without my uncle Murray? He was different from the entire family, tall, handsome, red-headed with a cleft in his chin and a twinkle in his eye, looking just like Robert Mitchum. Murray lived his life out loud, couldn't care less what anyone thought about him. He ran a successful plate-glass business, and loved horses and women, not in that exact order, either. Murray bet the horses regularly and made no bones about his other activities. The whole family looked away when he came into the room, but I liked him. When he came into a room, you could breathe. He filled it with fresh air.

I was proud of Murray for speaking out the truth, and always looked forward to hearing what he had to say. Murray saw that I was different from others in the family and took a liking to me as well.

"Honey," he once told me, "don't listen to what anyone tells you. There's only one sin in God's great world, and that's to lie. Remember that. Who are we to pretend to be someone we aren't?"

"Thanks, Uncle Murray, "I answered, "I'll remember."

Murray couldn't stand sanctimonious faces or special airs. Neither could I. Whenever he came to visit, I followed him wherever he went. One particular Sunday afternoon, he went out into the garden to have a smoke, while the family sat indoors, rolling their eyes.

"Let them sit there all day, judging everyone," Murray said, as I accompanied him outdoors. "God made us the way He made us. And I'd say He did a pretty damn good job. Who are we to improve on that?"

"No one, Uncle Murray," I answered.

He laughed. "You got it. We flash for a second like fireflies in the night, and then it's over, gets dark."

I knew what he meant. I loved watching fireflies light up the summer sky.

"Forget about listening to the dummies in there," Murray continued. "Better to sit out here and enjoy the beautiful afternoon."

When I put on plays that I wrote in the neighborhood Y, no one in the family came to see them except Uncle Murray. He drove all the way in from New Jersey to Brooklyn, with flowers in his hands. And he clapped the loudest when the curtain came down. After the show he'd run up onto the stage to hand me the bouquet.

"Hey, babe, you're my kind of woman," Murray would mutter. "It doesn't mean a damn that the others don't come. Who cares what they think? You're brave. That's what matters."

At that time Murray kept me going, single-handedly. He was brave and I craved bravery. Murray wouldn't let sly looks or secret messages pass by unnoticed, silently sinking into your heart, wreaking havoc. Whenever his wife, my aunt Rosie, was looking glum or giving him a fishy eye, he spoke right out.

"I'm not a guy who was made for just one woman, Rosie," he said, right in front of whoever was around. "God just didn't make me that way."

"I know that, Murray," Rosie would mumble.

"Take me as I am, or don't take me, "Murray belted out.

"I'll take you Murray, I'll take you," my aunt Rosie always replied.

Did Rosie have a good guy? I have no idea. But she certainly had one who was real. And she had no choice about it— Rosie loved Murray. She took him exactly as he was.

37

The Cop and the Convict

AS MY PRACTICE RIPENED, ONE day I was asked to teach a group of New York City transit authority policemen a class on self-change. These were tough guys who'd seen the worst of life, and to my great surprise, they loved the class, jumped right in. Many of them were practicing Catholics, but they seemed especially intrigued by the section on Zen.

So, besides just talking about it, I showed them how to sit and bow. Some laughed but others wanted more. They told me how they worked in Times Square and the kind of rough encounters they had over and over. What did their work have to do with bowing and sitting in zazen?

It was a great question, a natural koan, and I told them they'd have to answer it themselves, by sitting and bowing as much as they could. That didn't go over so well. They wanted me to give them an answer. I told them they had their own answers, inside.

In order to give them a firmer base in Zen practice, I arranged for them all to go to the zendo for beginner's instruction on a Thursday night. Of course, when they walked in, they'd have to take off their shoes and leave their guns at the door.

Zazen at the zendo was more strenuous and demanding than sitting in our class. At the zendo, the sittings lasted longer and the students could not move at all. A few enjoyed it. One did not. He said he'd rather get beaten up than sit so long without moving again.

There was one officer though, Tom, who was completely taken by the practice. He saw possibilities none of the other cops had thought of before.

The part that was most meaningful to him was the section on bowing—putting his hands together and making a small bow (gassho) to whoever was in front of him. We talked about it in class a few days later. Tom said it made him feel so different the minute he did that. It changed his mood and behavior quickly. I suggested he do it wherever he was. Before he arrested someone he could bow to that person in their mind, or even really do it. In that moment, he would be acknowledging the common humanity between him and the convict. Perhaps he would be prevented from inadvertently treating the person he was arresting too harshly then.

Most of the cops laughed, but Tom loved the idea. He wanted to get started on it right away. Next week he came back and reported that he tried it with a guy he was arresting and immediately, things turned around. He'd actually felt kindly toward the guy. And the person was easier to be with too. They'd both felt something.

Tom was flustered. He said, "After I bowed to this guy in

my mind, he calmed down and looked at me funny. And, for the first time, I saw a real person there. Instead of locking him up, I wanted to hug him. I can't get over it. How come?"

Of course the real person was always there, it was only that Tom's stopping and bowing, his taking the moment to be with this person differently, allowed him to see what was in front of his eyes. I then suggested that they all do it, at least for one week. They should bow in their minds to family, friends, someone they were about to get into a fight with. See what happened then.

Others tried it and came back with all kinds of reports. Some liked it, others thought it was creepy, most didn't really want to continue. It was too weird for them.

Tom, though, did it consistently, for longer than one week. This simple practice had great power in his life. His point of view about himself and others changed dramatically and he went on to get a master's degree in Tibetan Buddhist studies, along with becoming a student of Zen.

When we bow to someone in that manner, we are recognizing, uniting with and honoring the aliveness and truth that is common to all. Enemies can turn to friends quickly. Difficulties can melt away. Living in this manner, it is easy to see where true healing and support come from. Why not try and see?

In a moment of bowing, of honoring each other's humanity, making room for their lives and experience, who is the cop and who is the convict? Who is the one bowing to whom? With this attitude, not only the cop and the convict, but all so-called opponents can easily find a common ground. Take a moment to bow to your opponent, respect who he is, what he's gone through. Take a precious moment to look into his eyes without an agenda.

The simple question is do we want to? Are we willing to let go of our endless complaints, grudges and sense of self which is better and different from everyone? If we do, we do not lose anything, only gain the entire world.

All that it takes is a drop of willingness, and the ability to stop for a second or two. That second will grow on its own accord. That one second has the power to wrap itself around your heart and make all kinds of blossoms bloom where there was only dry land.

"The plum tree of my hut
It couldn't be helped,
It bloomed."

—Shiki

38

The World Calls Me

"A traveler,

May I thus be called,

This autumn evening."

—Basho

THE WORLD CALLS MY BROTHER Danny, every nook and cranny of it, every people, language, race. Not only does he speak many languages and read the literature of all peoples, he's lived everywhere on the earth. A fervently Orthodox Jew, he's made his home in a hammock in the Amazon, on the streets of Egypt, in all parts of Europe and South America.

"What do you do when you get there?" I always ask him, nervously. Since he was born we've been best friends. Very few days have passed when we haven't spoken.

"I enjoy myself," he always says with a grin. "Make new friends, expand my horizons, discover new worlds."

I, a natural homebody who loves sitting still in zazen for hours, shivers when he says that.

"You'll be careful?" I make him promise, as I know he travels off the grid, has a taste for odd places. "Do I have to worry?"

"Nothing to worry about, ever," he always answers, laughing, "God is with me wherever I go."

And it's true. Danny lives blessed and protected, a secret sage who gives whatever he has and brings love and goodwill to all he meets.

Living totally in the moment, Danny seldom knows where he's going until a day or two before takeoff or what he'll do when he arrives. Once, at a stopover in Iceland, he was so mesmerized by the beauty of the sky that he called me to send him a warm sweater. He'd let his plane fly off without him, couldn't bear to leave.

You never know when he's going, either. The moment comes, and he's called to explore. He takes almost nothing with him, either, his prayer books, Tefillin, and a couple of pieces of clothes. Wherever he goes, he mixes with the people, buys the clothing they wear, talks their language and very soon, finds a place to stay at someone's home.

Little by little, Danny has rid himself of more and more possessions. "It feels great, it feels wonderful," he reassures me. "Less baggage to carry around. Your baggage owns you, not the other way around. G-d didn't create us to accumulate junk."

Danny and I have spent hours upon hours discussing Judaism and Zen. As he keeps Jewish practice strongly and, to me, is one of the most learned men I have ever known; there's no end to what he knows about the depth of Torah and tells me constantly. It is both beautiful and agonizing for me to listen. Mostly, I respond quoting the teachings of Zen. But year after year I feel inadequate, awful, as if I'm missing something, doing life wrong. No matter how I've tried I'm not able to join him in his level of observance.

Then, suddenly, one day, my eyes opened wide.

More than anyone I've ever known, Danny is a Zen man. He lives a total Zen life—no attachments, few possessions, no plans, open to whatever the moment brings. He lives completely accepting of all people, his greatest joy being a true friend. So, here he is, practicing as an Orthodox Jew and living the Zen life in his flesh and bones.

And me, sitting in zazen for year upon year and yet great attachment to home and family, to caring for others—leading the life of a Jewish grandma!"

The bubble burst and I started laughing as Danny and I spoke on the phone.

"You're a Zen master," I finally told him, "living the life I'm only talking about."

He joined me in the laughter. "You're absolutely right," he said, "Our wires must have gotten crossed somehow."

"Or maybe all practices are one," I responded, "and we just do what we need to balance ourselves out."

"Maybe," he said, "but why speculate? Did you see how beautiful the sun was this afternoon?"

With Gratitude
(Sangha)

"For the sangha
Harmony is
Most precious."

—Soen Roshi

ITHOUT SANGHA, THE WONDERFUL COMMUNITY of students who gather to sit together, it may be impossible to go on. There are so many wonderful sangha friends who have contributed to each moment of practice and life. I deeply thank Haskel, Pawel, Jacques, Constantin, Martin, Peter, Bernie, Richard, Michael; the list goes on and on. We sit together and then have tea, sometimes in silence, sometimes in heated discussion, mirroring each other, silently lending the strength and inspiration to take the next breath, and march on.

When trouble came at the zendo, Haskel and I sat on a bench for what seemed like hours trying to make sense of everything. Coming from the same religious background, gripped by the same yearning for zazen, we endlessly explored the nuances of both practices, the ways they intersect, how to make our practice truly healing and whole. He is my neighbor as well as my dharma brother, and we do zazen, listen to talks, laugh, cry, sometimes celebrate the Sabbath and refuse to let either practice die.

Pawel has no conflict—about anything. He was there the moment I met the Roshi from Japan. Pawel sat through that sesshin and when he heard that the Roshi had invited me to come to Japan to practice with him, he vehemently insisted that I go.

"No excuses, no escapes," Pawel demanded, "just go and let the chips fall where they may."

An artist and dedicated Zen student, Pawel laughs at difficulty and whenever a stumbling block arises, jumps over it one way or another.

"Go deeper in this book," he demanded, when I asked him to read it. "No stone unturned, no page cluttered. Make it balanced, find compassion for everyone! Otherwise, what is it? Just more propaganda and lack of balance."

For almost thirty years, Jacques has always been there on the cushion, just a few breaths away. After I returned from Japan and moved out of the city, Jacques took a long bus ride to come and sit with me in my new home. Seems we always sit together, wherever I am. Solid, warm, stable, kind and non-swerving, Jacques asks for little, gives much, and is grateful for each moment, and for each chance to practice together.

Different sangha members become closer at different periods. These days Constantin, tall and dedicated, has turned into a mountain beside me, sitting fiercely. He practices alone intensively to prepare for our long sits the last Friday of each month. Constantin brings with him the atmosphere of the monastery and all that is possible—unflinching in every way.

Peter and I sat together more in the earlier days. Each summer we went to a barn in the back of a friend's pottery studio and held a weekend sesshin. It was a small space, large enough originally for two horses. In the back was a beautiful bamboo garden, a few steps away from the ocean. We called it Tropicana Sesshin, as the two of us sat together, from morning to night, serving Tropicana orange juice instead of green tea. We did kinhin in the bamboo garden and also down at the beach in the evening. Zazen planted in natural gardens with just one dear dharma friend—more than enough to carry on.

Peter studied with Kyudo Roshi. After Kyudo Roshi returned to Japan, Peter kept the zendo open for many years, almost single-handedly. Every week he'd drive in from East Hampton, where he then lived, opened the door and ran the evening sitting. He'd be there year after year, even though many times only one person, or no one, came. It didn't matter. When the time for zazen came, he'd ring the bell and sit.

Bernie, Richard and Michael are regulars here on Monday nights, though there is nothing at all to get but the practice of zazen. In our little home-grown zendo there are no teachers, no teachings, just sitting together, dedicating our sitting to those in need. And then, at the perfect moment, sharing slices of oranges, bananas and pears.

We come together from different backgrounds and affiliations. Bernie, a psychologist and gerontologist as well as a reporter, is the author of *Jesus Uncensored, Restoring the Authentic Jew*.

Richard, who spent years in India, is the official biographer of the Jalalamudi mother, writing the beautiful book *The Mother of All*, along with other spiritual biographies.

Michael, an incredible artist and musician, is faithful in his love for practice and supporting those with whom he sits.

To these and many others who have shared their love, I bow in deep gratitude.

"Apples given
And oranges received
In return."

—Shiki

Resources

Cover photo is by Pawel Wojtasik, www.pawelwojtasik.com

Cover design by Ilan Kwittken, ilanmarc@msn.com

Photo of Brenda Eshin Shoshanna by
adamlukeman@gmail.com, www.adamlukeman.com

Contact Brenda Eshin Shoshanna at
brendashoshanna@gmail.com,
www.grabthedustrag.com
www.drshoshanna.com

Thanks to my wonderful copy editor Christine LePorte

Made in the USA
Middletown, DE
26 September 2018